COMPUTER SECURITY:
FROM PASSWORDS TO
BEHAVIORAL BIOMETRICS

COMPUTER SECURITY: FROM PASSWORDS TO BEHAVIORAL BIOMETRICS

ROMAN V. YAMPOLSKIY, PhD
University of London

New Academic Publishing
London, UK

COMPUTER SECURITY: FROM PASSWORDS TO BEHAVIORAL BIOMETRICS

COPYRIGHT (c) 2008 Roman V. Yampolskiy, New Academic Publishing

ISBN: 978-0-6152-1818-2

To My Mother and Father

Table of Contents

LIST OF TABLES

LIST OF FIGURES

LIST OF ABBREVIATIONS

AI	Artificial Intelligence
AIS	Artificial Immune System
ART	Adaptive Resonance Theory
ASCII	American Standard Code for Information Interchange
ATT	Automated Turing Test
BB	Behavioral Biometrics
BBID	Behavior Based Intrusion Detection
BCI	Brain Computer Interface
C4.5	Decision Tree
CAPTCHA	Completely Automated Public Turing test to tell Computer and Humans Apart
COPS	Check-Off Password System
CPU	Central Processing Unit
DARPA	Defense Advanced Research Project Agency
DOS	Denial of Service
DSL	Digital Subscriber Line
DVD	Digital Video Disk
EER	Equal Error Rate
FAR	False Accept Rate
FRR	False Reject Rate
GAU	Gaussian Classifier
GMAT	Graduate Management Admission Test
GRE	Graduate Record Examination
GUI	Graphical User Interface
HCI	Human Computer Interaction
HIP	Human Interactive Proof
HIS	Human Immune System
HMM	Hidden Markov Model
HYP	Hyper Sphere Algorithm
I/O	Input/Output
ID	Intrusion Detection
IDS	Intrusion Detection System
IIDS	Intelligent Intrusion Detection System
IP	Internet Protocol
IQ	Intelligence Quotient
IRBF	Incremental Radial Basis Function
ISP	Internet Service Provider
KDD	Knowledge Discovery and Data mining
K-M	K-Means clustering

LEA	Leader Algorithm
MBB	Multi-modal Behavioral Biometrics
MHP	Mandatory Human Participation
MHZ	Mega Hertz
MLP	Multiple Layer Perceptron
MMORPG	Massive Multiplayer Online Role-Playing Game
NEA	Nearest Cluster Algorithm
NN	Neural Network
NP	Nondeterministic Polynomial
NPC	Non-Playing Character
OS	Operating System
PB	Physical Biometrics
R2L	Remote-to-Local
RAD	Registry Anomaly Detection
RAM	Random Access Memory
RBF	Radial Basis Function Network
ROC	Receiver Operating Characteristics
RTT	Reverse Turing Test
SAN	Storage Area Network
SAT	Scholastic Aptitude Test
SNN	Shared Nearest Neighbor
SOM	Self Organizing Maps
T1	Digital Signal 1
TCP	Transmission Control Protocol
U2R	User-to-Root
UDP	User Datagram Protocol
UMI	Unit of Memorable Information
UNIX	UNiplexed Information and Computing System
USB	Universal Serial Bus

PREFACE

This book is a review of published research in computer security, user authentication, intrusion detection, game security and behavioral biometrics. We analyze previous studies and point out trends and propose taxonomies which make understanding and improvement on previous work easier. In particular the majority of contributions in this book is to the field of behavioral biometrics. Research in biometric technologies offers one of the most promising approaches to providing user friendly and reliable control methodology for access to computer systems, networks and workplaces. Majority of such research is aimed at studying well established physical biometrics such as fingerprint or iris recognition. Behavioral biometrics are usually only briefly mentioned and only those which are in large part based on muscle control such as keystrokes, gait or signature are well investigated. This book was written to fill the coverage gap with respect to this promising technology.

Additionally the book covers our investigatation of the existing authentication schemas and after analysis of their shortcomings proposes a number of behavior-based user authentication methodologies aimed at improving the currently dominant password-based approach. We also describe a novel CAPTCHA-based algorithm aimed at preventing intelligent agents from participating in online games. Furthermore the book describes an intrusion detection system based on indirect behavioral biometrics which uses neural networks instead of statistical profiling to achieve its goals. In its final chapter the book outlines some future directions for research in behavioral biometrics and security.

Keywords: *Authentication, Behavioral Biometrics, Behavioral Profiling, Biometric Signature, Bots, CAPTCHA, Cheating, Computer Security, Game Security, Graphical Password, Human Computer Interaction, Indirect Biometrics, Intrusion Detection, Intruder, Motor Control, Multiple Layer Perceptron, Muscle Control, Network Traffic, Neural Networks, PassMap, PassText, Password, Poker, Radial Basis Function Network, Taxonomy, User Identification, User Verification.*

CHAPTER 1 - INTRODUCTION

"The beginning of knowledge is the discovery of something we do not understand"

Frank Herbert (1920 - 1986)

Abstract—*this chapter presents an introduction as well as a brief description of our work. It outlines the research area, states initial objectives of our research and serves as the reader's guide to the entire book. Significant contributions of this book are highlighted and described. Research papers which make up the body of this book are introduced and placed in the context of chapters based on them.*

1. INTRODUCTION

This book is a review of published research in computer security, user authentication, intrusion detection, game security and behavioral biometrics. We analyze previous studies and point out trends and propose taxonomies which make understanding and improvement on previous work easier. In particular majority of contributions in this book is to the field of behavioral biometrics. Research in biometric technologies offers one of the most promising approaches to providing user friendly and reliable control methodology for access to computer systems, networks and workplaces. Majority of such research is aimed at studying well established physical biometrics such as fingerprint or iris recognition. Behavioral biometrics are usually only briefly mentioned and only those which are in large part based on muscle control such as keystrokes, gait or signature are well investigated. This book was written to fill the coverage gap with respect to this promising technology.

Additionally the book covers our investigatation of the existing authentication schemas and after analysis of their shortcomings proposes a number of behavior-based user authentication methodologies aimed at improving the currently dominant password-based approach. We also describe a novel CAPTCHA-based algorithm aimed at preventing intelligent agents from participating in online games. Furthermore the book describes an intrusion detection system based on indirect behavioral biometrics which uses neural networks instead of statistical profiling to achieve its goals. In its final chapter the book outlines some future directions for research in behavioral biometrics and security.

2. BOOK STRUCTURE AND CONTRIBUTIONS

In this book we have analyzed hundreds of research papers on the topics of computer security, intrusion detection, game security and behavioral biometrics. As a product of our analysis we have created a number of surveys, novel taxonomies and classifications helping us and interested readers to better understand current state-of-the-art in those fields:

Chapter	Type	Topic	Details
2	Survey	Computer Security	a meta survey of existing surveys
3	Overview	Game Security	includes a section on game bots
3	Overview	Bot Prevention	lists popular anti-bot approaches
4	Taxonomy	Behavioral Biometrics	definitions for the five basic types
5	Survey	User Authentication	graphical and textual approaches
6	Review	Password Dictionaries	includes approaches presented by us

Table 1.1: Surveys, taxonomies and classifications of prior work

Our research has resulted in a number of contributions to such diverse areas as computer security, behavioral biometrics, intrusion detection systems, and human-computer disambiguation. Following is a list of the most important contributions which is further described in the following section and respective chapters of the book:

- Designed an embedded continuous non-interactive CAPTCHA algorithm
- Designed authentication schemas based on behavior and knowledge of the user combining graphical and textual approaches
- Demonstrated that properly trained neural networks are capable of fast recognition and classification of different attacks based on the flow of network data
- Compared performance of MLP and RBF neural networks with respect to security applications
- Presented our view of the future of the behavioral biometrics

The book is based on research previously published in peer-reviewed workshops, conferences and journals. Each chapter is written as an independent self-contained research article with its own goals, experiments and conclusions as overviewed in the following table.

Chapter	Research Type	Title	Published as:
1	-	- Introduction	n/a
2	Survey	- Computer Security	[456]
3	Survey/ Experiment	- Online Poker Security Problems and Solutions	[444, 443, 452, 448, 459]
4	Taxonomy	- Behavioral Biometrics	[449, 450, 451, 455, 457]
5	Survey/ Research	- Comparison of PassText, PassArt and PassMap for User Authentication	[453, 454, 445]
6	Survey/ Theory	- Analyzing User Password Selection Behavior for Reduction of Password Space	[440]
7	Experiment	- Traffic Analysis Based Identification of Network Attacks	[325, 326]
8	Theory	- Behavioral Biometrics – Future Directions	[442]
9	-	- Bibliography	n/a

Table 1.2: Book chapters and our publications they are based on

Chapter 2 reviews research papers which survey all aspects of computer security including attackers and attacks, software bugs and viruses as well as different intrusion detection systems and ways to evaluate such systems. The aim is to develop a survey of security related issues which provides adequate information and advice to newcomers to the field as well as a good reference guide for security professionals. This survey was initially made public as *"Computer Security: a Survey of Methods and Systems"* [456].

Chapter 3 continues with the security theme and is concerned with cheating in online computer games.We review different forms of cheating observed in computer games and solutions developed to counteract different forms of cheating. Finally, we give our own solution to one particular form of cheating, which involves assistance from artificially intelligent programs (bots). Our solution has advantages such as its non-obtrusive nature, continuous verification, and simple non-interactive and outsourcing-proof design. The work in this chapter was first presented in *"Embedded CAPTCHA for Online Poker"* [444] followed by *"Online Poker Security: Problems and Solutions"* [452], *"Graphical*

CAPTCHA embedded in cards" [448], *"Embedded Non-Interactive Continuous Bot Detection"* [459], and *"Detecting and Controlling Cheating in Online Poker"* [443].

Chapter 4 surveys the state of the art in behavioral biometrics based on skills, style, preference, knowledge, motor-skills or strategy used by people while accomplishing different everyday tasks such as driving an automobile, writing an email message or using a computer. We examine current research and analyze the types of features, compare accuracy rates for verification of users using different behavioral approaches and address privacy issues. This chapter is based on the following papers: *"Indirect Human Computer Interaction-Based Biometrics for Intrusion Detection Systems"* [450], *"Motor-Skill Based Biometrics"* [451], *"Behavioral Biometrics: a Survey and Classification"* [455], *"Direct and Indirect Human Computer Interaction Based Biometrics"* [457] and *"Human Computer Interaction Based Intrusion Detection"* [449].

Chapter 5 compares password-like user authentication approaches. Network security partially depends on reliable user authentication; unfortunately currently used passwords are not completely secure. One of the main problems is that good passwords are hard to remember and the ones which are easy to remember are too simple to be secure. We have designed authentication schemas, which are easy to remember and can be relatively quickly provided to the system, while at the same time remain impossible to break with brute force alone. In this chapter we have compared the size of password spaces and how easy they are to remember for popular alphanumeric and graphical authentication schemas against our approaches. Namely PassText, PassArt and PassMap. This chapter summarizes three of our publications: *"User Authentication via Behavior Based Passwords"* [454], *"Secure Network Authentication with PassText"* [453] and *"Enhanced Passwords for Improved Network Security"* [445].

Chapter 6 presents a comprehensive survey of recent literature on the topic of password dictionaries for alphanumeric and graphical user authentication approaches including some password schemas proposed by us. After different methods used for reduction of password space are introduced, they are analyzed and compared with the intent of finding a common flaw of user authentication mechanisms, which allows for the development of such password dictionaries by hackers. We conclude that any user authentication system, which allows users to exercise choice in selection of their passwords, is vulnerable to the password space reduction methods presented. This chapter is based on our paper *"Analyzing User Password Selection Behavior for Reduction of Password Space"* [440].

Chapter 7 is devoted to the problem of identification of network attacks via traffic analysis. We show that properly trained neural networks are capable of fast recognition and classification of different attacks. Our approach allows us to demonstrate the superiority of the neural networks due to their capability to recognize an attack, to differentiate one attack from another, i.e. classify attacks and to detect new attacks that were not included in the training set. The research in this chapter has been previously made available by us as: "*Anomaly Detection Based Intrusion Detection*" [325] and "*Artificial Intelligence Approaches for Intrusion Detection*" [326].

Chapter 8 begins with an overview of a multidisciplinary problem of behavior profiling. It looks at possible applications of such technology and proposes new directions for research. From the security point of view the chapter proposes and explores some novel behavioral biometrics and research paths as well as some universal descriptors of behavior in general. It concludes with an analysis of how behavior can be influenced by the environment in particular location of an individual. An interested reader is encouraged to read "*Behavioral Modeling: an Overview*" [442].

CHAPTER 2 - COMPUTER SECURITY

"The ultimate security is your understanding of reality"

H. Stanley Judd

Abstract—*In this chapter we review papers which survey all aspects of computer security including attackers and attacks, software bugs and viruses as well as different intrusion detection systems and ways to evaluate such systems. The aim was to develop a survey of security related issues which would provide adequate information and advice to newcomers to the field as well as a good reference guide for security professionals.*

1. INTRODUCTION

As computer systems become more and more important to our every day lives it is necessary to protect them from actions that attempt to compromise the reliability, confidentiality or availability of such systems [19, 235]. In the context of information systems, intrusion refers to any unauthorized access or malicious use of information resources [214, 327]. Intrusion Detection (ID) is defined as detection of break-ins and break-in attempts via automated software system [460].

Intrusion detection systems can be grouped into two broad categories: knowledge-based or behavior-based [225, 221, 418, 98]. Majority of currently deployed systems are knowledge-based, matching signatures of well-known attacks against state changes in systems or in streams of packets flowing through the network [70, 119]. Knowledge-based systems are reliable and generate very few false positives, but they can only detect intrusions, which are similar to the ones previously encountered [80]. Such systems are powerless against new, as of yet unknown attacks, so they must be continually updated with information about new types of attacks being utilized by hackers [460]. Recently, a trend of incorporating different AI technologies into Intrusion Detection Systems (IDS) has demonstrated promising results particularly with agent-based systems [162, 35, 416].

Behavior Based Intrusion Detection (BBID) is also known as anomaly detection [118] and statistical intrusion detection [261]. The first step of a BBID system is to learn what behavior is normal. When a BBID system is activated for the first time, it will monitor and log a number of user parameters such as: bandwidth usage, processor and memory activity, disk usage, and other system activity over a certain period to create a baseline of what constitutes normal behavior. Activity that doesn't match to the normal results in an alert signal. The advantage is that it dynamically adapts to new types of attacks. Because system behavior can fluctuate during use for normal reasons, it typically produces a large number of false alarms [460].

As was previously mentioned behavior-based approaches can detect even unforeseen vulnerabilities. They can even contribute to the automatic discovery of these new attacks. They are also less dependent on operating system-specific attack approaches. They detect internal-abuse types of attacks that do not actually involve exploiting any security vulnerability, but rely on privileges already possessed by the users to obtain additional control over the system. BBID system is basically an obsessed approach: Everything which has not been seen previously is classified as some type of an attack [460].

The high false alarm rate is the primary drawback of BBID system because the entire spectrum of the behavior of the user may not be encountered during the learning phase. Since behavior can change over time, there is a need for periodic online retraining of the behavioral profile. This additional training may result either in unavailability of the BBID system or in additional false alarms being generated. The system we are trying to protect can also be under attack while the BBID system is in learning mode. Consequently, the behavioral profile will contain intrusive behavior, which is not detected as anomalous during the utilization of BBID system [460].

2. REQUIREMENTS OF A TAXONOMY

Research in computer security is an area of investigation which can benefit from a systematic classification and analysis. Some of the first attempts at analyzing state of computer security research appeared long before prevalence of the personal computer [42]. C. Meadows presented a taxonomy of computer security research and development intended to spot areas of research which are still relatively unexplored [301]. It includes five broad areas: systems, policies, techniques, assurance and interaction with other system requirements.

Lundin et al. presented a survey which focuses on different issues which must be addressed in order to build a fully functional and practical IDS [285]. The survey focuses on social aspects, foundations, data collection, detection methods, response, environment and architecture, IDS security, testing, evaluation, and operational aspects. In general, a good taxonomy has a number of desirable properties as outlined by Hansman [186]:

- **Accepted** The taxonomy should be structured so that it can become generally approved.
- **Comprehensible** A comprehensible taxonomy will be able to be understood by those who are in the security field, as well as those who only have an interest in it.
- **Complete** For the taxonomy to be exhaustive, it should account for possible attacks and provide categories accordingly.
- **Deterministic** The procedure of classifying must be clearly defined.
- **Mutually exclusive** Each attack is categorized into, at most, one category.
- **Repeatable** Classification should be repeatable.
- **Backwards compatible** Existing terminology should be used in the taxonomy so as to avoid confusion and to build on previous knowledge.
- **Terms well defined** There should be no confusion at to what a term means.
- **Unambiguous** Each category of the taxonomy must be well defined so there is no ambiguity with respect to an attack's classification.
- **Useful** A useful taxonomy will be able to be used in the security industry and particularly by incident response teams.

3. INTRUSION DETECTION SYSTEMS, TECHNOLOGIES AND PRODUCTS

The different IDS taxonomies are so numerous that meta-studies of such classification systems began to appear [39, 372]. Debar et al. developed taxonomy which defines families of intrusion detection systems according to their properties [138]. The main categories used in their classification are detection method, behavior on detection, audit source location, and usage frequency. They have later extended their taxonomy beyond real-time intrusion detection to include additional aspects of security monitoring, such as vulnerability assessment [137].

S. Axelsson developed a taxonomy which consists of a classification based on detection principle and operational aspects of the IDS [50]. The detection principles are divided into anomaly, signature, and signature-inspired. The system characteristic categories considered are time of detection, granularity of data processing, source of audit data, response to detected intrusions, locus of data processing, locus of data collection, security and degree of interoperability.

Lazarevic et al. developed a taxonomy of IDS based on five criteria: information source (system commands, system accounting, system log, security audit processing, network packets, application log files), analysis strategy, time aspects, architecture, and response type [262].

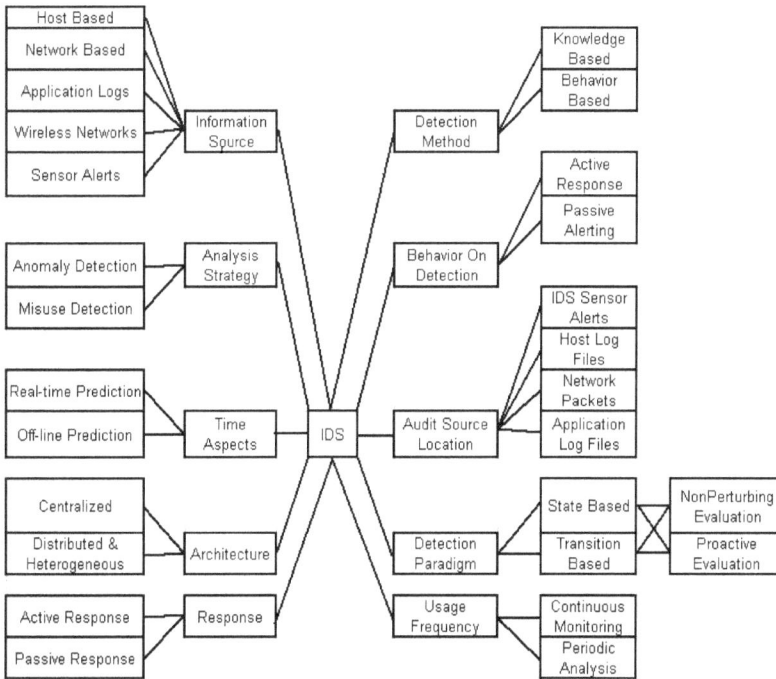

Figure 2.1: Left: IDS classification by Debar et al. (based on [137]); Right: IDS taxonomy by Lazarevic (based on [262])

Many other IDS surveys and taxonomies have been put forward:

- Allesandri et al. developed a taxonomy of IDS with respect to the analysis of activities such as attacks and other related events [38]. The attributes are classified into three categories: generic characteristics, data preprocessing, and instance analysis.

- Xiao et al. classify the architectures of IDS that have been developed for mobile ad hoc networks [41].

- Michael Treaster describes different approaches that have been developed to share and analyze data in distributed IDS [400].

Almgren et al. has attempted to compare classification terms used in different IDS surveys as show in Table 2.1.

Author	Terms used in Survey		
Halme and Bauer	Anomaly		Misuse
Debar et al.	Behavior-based		Knowledge-Based
Ko	Anomaly	Specification-based	Missuse
Lindqvist	Dynamic knowledge Default deny		Static knowledge Default permit
Axelssson	Anomaly Self-Learned	Signature-inspired	Signature Programmed
MAFTIA	No corresponding mapping		

Table 2.1: Terms used in different taxonomies to classify IDS (taken from [39])

3.1 INTRUSION RESPONSE

Increased complexity of attacks in recent years coupled with high speed at which attacks propagate requires an automated intrusion response mechanism to be included with the modern IDS [295, 411]. Stakhanova et al. developed taxonomy of intrusion response systems [388]. Systems are classified based on the degree of automation, the activity of triggered response, ability to adjust, time of response, cooperation ability and response selection method.

Carver et al. proposed an intrusion response taxonomy consisting of six layers including: timing of attack, type of attack, type of attacker, degree of suspicion, attack implications and environmental constraints [103]. They suggest that a response to an attack should be customized with respect to each of these subcategories.

Jayaram et al. present a taxonomic view of network security [217]. They quantify the classes of security threats and mechanisms for meeting these security threats. They identify five ways in which network security can be compromised including: physical, system weak spots, malign programs, access rights, and communication channels.

3.2 ALARM CORRELATION

Many IDS are complementary to each other and are used in combination. Alert correlation methods help to discern between positive and false alarms generated by such multi-IDS approaches. Zurutuza et al. present a survey of intrusion detection alarm correlation approaches [475]. Reviewed methods for alarm correlation include: probabilistic alarm correlation, method of duplicates and consequences, and predicate logic based approaches.

3.3 IMMUNE SYSTEMS

Artificial Immune Systems (AIS) are inspired by the Human Immune System (HIS) which protects the body against damage from bacteria and viruses [370]. It is hoped that an AIS can protect computer systems against computer viruses in a similar fashion. Dasgupta et al. present a survey of different AIS algorithms and numerous applications of this technology to computer security, anomaly detection in data, and fault diagnosis [134]. They review computational models such as: Immune Network Model and Negative Selection Algorithm. Similarly, Aickelin et al. [33] evaluate systems based on: gene libraries, negative selection, clonal selection, immune memory, idotypic networks, and self-nonself detection.

3.4 STORAGE SYSTEMS SECURITY

Storage networks utilized to keep and share sensitive data such as healthcare records, and financial transactions are vulnerable to security breeches. Kher et al. presented a comprehensive survey of the security services provided by the existing storage systems [237]. Such services include authentication and authorization, availability, confidentiality and integrity, key management, auditing and intrusion detection as well as usability, manageability and performance. They survey networked file systems (Andrew file systems, self-certifying file systems, and network attached storage devices), cryptographic file systems (shared and non-shared cryptographic systems) and storage-based IDS (self-securing storage, storage-based IDS).

3.5 IDS-PRODUCT REVIEW

While a great number of theoretical surveys and classification schemas of IDS have been published a much smaller effort has been devoted to the review of actual commercially available IDS. K. Jackson developed a comprehensive compilation and categorization of commercially available IDS [205]. The survey is based on published reports, product evaluations and vendor-supplied product information. Assessment of seventeen different systems is performed in terms of detection method, suitability, flexibility, support, performance and accuracy. In a very similar work, H. Kvarnstrom reviews commercially available tools for detecting intrusions in computer systems and networks [254]. Systems are compared and evaluated with respect to functioning, security, architecture, performance and manageability.

In a larger study, S. Axelsson classifies 20 different intrusion detection systems based on a taxonomy of system features developed by the author [51]. The systems are reviewed in chronological order with each review followed by the systems' evolution from the surveyor. Allen et al. presented an assessment of publicly available intrusion detection technology [37]. The report provides recommendations for IDS sponsors, users, vendors and researchers. It recommends: creation of open source signatures, utilization of distribution model similar to the one used by anti-virus community, integration of human analysis as part of event diagnosis and expanding options for capturing forensic evidence.

A large number of smaller product surveys deserve to be mentioned:

- Krugel et al. survey thirteen existing IDS and describe current state-of-the art architectures and methods used to construct those systems [249].
- T. Lunt surveys different well known IDS from the point of view of automated audit trail analysis techniques [287].
- McAuliffe et al. performed a survey of the state-of-the-art in IDS [299].
- P. Raju overviews the state-of-the-art in IDS products and technologies in particular evaluating six commercially available intrusion detection systems [332].
- NATO research and technology organization produced a technical report on state-of-the-art IDS which includes review of some commercial and freeware products [125].

4. INTRUSION, ATTACKS, ATTACKERS, FLAWS AND VIRUSES

As technology advances so does the sophistication of attacks which can be generated by a relatively inexperienced attacker given he has access to the right set of tools. In order to improve accuracy in incident reporting, statistics, and warning bulletins Lindqvist et al. developed a classification of computer intrusions with respect to technique as well as result [279]. Three main subclasses of intrusions are presented: bypass of intended controls, active misuse of resources, and passive misuse of resources. Each type of intrusion may result in exposure of data, or denial of service or erroneous output. Alternatively, S. Kumar presented a classification of computer intrusions based on classifying signatures that are used to detect the exploitation or vulnerability [252].

4.1 ATTACKERS

Intruders themselves can be classified into different types [42]:

- **External intruders** don't have any type of authorized access to the system
- **Masqueraders** use authentication of other users to obtain corresponding privileges
- **Misfeasors** those are legitimate users who have privileged access to the system and abuse it to violate security policies [117, 340]
- **Clandestine users** access the system with supervisory privileges and operate at a level below a normal audit mechanism, making it very difficult to detect them

4.2 ATTACKS

Hansman et al. propose a four dimensional vector for attack classification [186]. The first dimension being the class of an attack such as: denial of service, password attack, physical attack, or information gathering attack. Second dimension is the target of an attack such as Windows based systems. The third dimension deals with vulnerabilities and exploits that the attack uses. The fourth dimension considers any payload an attack may include such as a virus that installs a Trojan horse program.

D. Alessandri developed a classification of attacks and a description framework for intrusion detection systems [36]. This method can be used to predict whether a given design will be able to detect certain classes of attacks. Attacks are classified according to their externally observable characteristics. The identified attack classes are then described in terms of IDS characteristics which are needed to analyze a given class of attacks.

Buhan et al. developed a meta-classification schema of attack taxonomies to provide guidance to the process of choosing the most suitable taxonomy for a security task [93]. They classify atomic taxonomies based on the grounds of distinction including:

- **The who** Classifies attacks based on different characteristics of an attacker.

- **The how** Groups attacks based on the attack method used.
- **The what** Arranges attacks based on the flaw being exploited.

Buhan's meta-taxonomy uses one taxonomy from each of the identified classes and by doing so allows for identification of a broad range of attacks [93]. Practically all of the well known attack taxonomies [290, 395, 323, 238, 199, 305, 387, 40, 24] can be classified according to this methodology.

4.3 VULNERABILITIES AND FLAWS

A good taxonomy of system vulnerabilities can help in detection and elimination of flaws from the current and future systems. Bishop presented a taxonomy of Unix vulnerabilities classified according to the following properties [74]:

- **Nature** The type of the flaw by genesis
- **Time of introduction** When the vulnerability was introduced
- **Exploitation domain** Where the vulnerability occurs
- **Effect domain** What is affected by the vulnerability
- **Minimum number** The minimum number of components needed to exploit the flaw

Additionally Bishop et al. [75] perform a critical analysis of other vulnerability taxonomies to define what makes a taxonomy good. T. Aslam also proposes a taxonomy of security faults in the Unix operating system [47]. His taxonomy includes such categories as: operational faults, coding faults, and environment faults all of which are subdivided into additional categories. Landwehr et al. developed taxonomy of computer program security flaws based on three broad classes, namely: genesis, time of introduction and location [258]. A number of other less known surveys of vulnerabilities and flaws also exist which tend to follow classification approaches similar to the ones described above [248, 404, 419, 47].

4.4 WORMS, VIRUSES AND TROJAN HORSES

The following definitions for different malicious software are generally accepted by the security research community [231, 154]:

- A virus is a self-replicating malicious program which relies on a careless user or other programs to replicate itself.
- A worm is a stand alone self-replicating program which uses vulnerability in the target's code to spread itself.

- Trojan horse is a program performing unknown and unwanted actions, while posing as a legitimate program. It can be equated to a non-replicating virus or a super-class for viruses and worms.

Weaver at el. [424] proposed a taxonomy of malicious worms based on target discovery and selection strategies, worm carrier mechanisms, worm activation, possible payloads, and plausible attackers who might utilize worms. M. Karresand has developed a comprehensive taxonomy of different software weapons which he defines as "...software containing instructions that are necessary and sufficient for a successful attack on a computer system". The taxonomy consists of 15 categories, which are independent and therefore may be used together to categorize any software weapon [231, 230]. Each category is further subdivided into 2-4 subgroups making it possible to accurately classify different malware.

4.5 DECEPTION IN CYBERSPACE

Deception is a valuable component of information warfare. Examples include many social engineering attacks such as: phishing [106] and "Nigerian letters". N. Rowe presented taxonomy of deception in cyberspace [353]. He enumerates the space of possible deceptions using a new approach derived from semantics in linguistics and rates appropriateness of each of the deceptions for offense and defense in cyberwar. His taxonomy includes such categories as: space, time, participant, causality, quality, and essence.

5. ANTI-TAMPER TECHNOLOGIES: WATERMARKING AND OBFUSCATION

Collberg et al. review several approaches for technical protection of software secrets which might be revealed as a result of software reverse engineering. While advocating software obfuscation as the best approach they also consider sale of services instead of application, code encryption, and native code only distribution. Software obfuscation refers to making the internals of a program unintelligible to a hacker by artificially changing the structure of the program, modifying span of variables, introducing new classes and methods, and increasing the number of arguments to a method [122].

Protection of copyrighted digital material may be accomplished by digital watermarking. It allows incorporation of a hidden verification message to digital audio, video, or image files. Shoemaker presents a survey of techniques used for digital watermarking including spatial, frequency and wavelet domain based approaches [374].

Atallah et al. present a general survey of multiple anti-tamper technologies [48]. They review both hardware and software based methods of protecting software from unauthorized access, reverse engineering, and violation of code's integrity. Examined hardware approaches include trusted processors, smart cards and tokens. Software methods such as encryption wrappers, code obfuscation, guarding, digital watermarking and fingerprinting are also evaluated.

6. EVALUATION OF SECURITY TOOLS

New ways of defending computer systems and networks against attacks are being continouly introduced. However, adaptation of novel approaches is only possible if they can be thoroughly evaluated and appropriate recommendations made with regard to their use. Molsa describes taxonomy of criteria for evaluating defense mechanisms against denial of service attacks [308]. Criteria such as effectiveness during normal activity and attack, ability to fulfill requirements on application quality of service, robustness against misuse, resilience against changes in attack characteristics, configuration capabilities, and interoperability are considered.

Kaiser et al. put forth a taxonomy for a usability evaluation of security tools [227]. The proposed taxonomy ranks security functions according to the user's ability to avoid self-induced, security-critical user errors and explains possible causes of such errors. Mell et al. explore the types of performance measurements that are effective at evaluating intrusion detection systems, such as: coverage, probability of false alarms, probability of detection, resistance to attacks directed at IDS, ability to handle high bandwidth traffic, correlate events, detect novel attacks, identify an attack, and determine attack success [302].

7. CONCLUSIONS

As computers and computer networks infiltrate every aspect of our society, computer security attracts considerable resources from both the research community and from commercial companies. In all likelihood, no IDS will ever be capable of accurately identifying every event occurring on any particular system [412]. The increasing complexity and rapid evolution of modern computer systems prevents realization of absolute security. We can however hope that our intrusion detection systems will allow for reduction in the number of successful computer attacks [456].

In this chapter we have reviewed papers which survey all aspects of computer security including attackers and attacks, software bugs and viruses as well as different intrusion detection systems and ways to evaluate such systems. The aim was to develop a survey of security related issues which would provide adequate information and advice to newcomers to the field as well as a good reference guide for security professionals.

CHAPTER 3 - ONLINE POKER SECURITY PROBLEMS AND SOLUTIONS

"Of course the game is rigged. Don't let that stop you—if you don't play, you can't win"

Robert Heinlein (1907 – 1988)

Abstract— *Cheating in online computer games is becoming a significant problem as the popularity of such games steadily increases. As a result, it costs thousands of dollars to game designers in lost revenue from disillusioned players who stop participating and in man-hours used for prevention of different forms of cheating. In this chapter we review different forms of cheating observed in computer games. This is followed by a review of solutions developed to counteract different forms of cheating. Finally, we give our solution for a particular form of cheating, which involves assistants from artificially intelligent programs, known as bots. Our solution has numerous advantages over traditional methods for combating this form of cheatin. It is non-obtrusive, offers continuous verification, and simple design.*

1. INTRODUCTION

Multiplayer online computer games are quickly growing in popularity with millions of players logging on every day. With the growth in the economic and social importance of the virtual game worlds cheating is becoming increasingly problematic [87], as it makes games less interesting for the honest players. It costs thousands of dollars to game designers in lost revenue from disillusioned players who stop participating and in man-hours used for prevention of different forms of cheating. Consequently, a great deal of current research in computer science has been aimed at detecting, preventing and neutralizing cheating in game worlds [226, 104, 112, 63, 271]. Cheating is also being investigated by researchers in media sciences to analyze the social, ethical and moral aspects of cheating [160, 159, 250, 378, 253, 375, 189].

2. SECURITY ISSUES IN COMPUTER GAMES

2.1 WHAT IS CHEATING?

Cheating in games can be defined as "any behavior that a player uses to gain an advantage over his peer players or achieve a target in an online game ... if, according to the game rules or at the discretion of the game operator (the game service provider, who is not necessarily the developer of the game), the advantage or the target is one that he is not supposed to have achieved" [464, 465]. Players themselves classify cheating into three often overlapping categories [124]:

- **Anything except unaided play** Using strategy guides, walkthroughs, cheat codes and hacking is all cheating.
- **Code tampering** Any modifications to the source code of the game is considered to be cheating.
- **Cheating other players** The strictest definition which says that cheating takes place only if another player is disadvantaged as a result of the cheaters actions.

A game cheat has many motives such as: obtaining free play, stealing virtual resources, completing otherwise difficult game quests, getting stuck, speeding up action, becoming a famous hacker, sabotaging the game provider out of revenge or jealousy, or acquiring virtual resources for sale in the real world [288, 124]. Rule violations can be classified based on who is being the victim. While an attack against multiple targets is feasible, three distinct targets are suggested by Lyhyaoui et al. [288]:

- **Provider** A cheating attack against the game provider includes violation of implicit or explicit contract between the player as a customer and game developer as a service provider. Players may cheat the provider out of subscription fees for the service via the use of stolen credit cards. Colluding players may engage in theft of service via account sharing and so reduce the profitability of developing and running a game. In general, cheating players undermine the confidence of other players in the game's security and so reduce profitability for the game developer because of the reduced enrollment.
- **Players** The most frequent object of an attack is honest players. Almost all attacks described in this chapter are of this type of target. Their money and virtual assets may be stolen, accounts compromised and overall enjoyment of the game experience ruined.
- **Virtual society** The moral rules which allow the virtual community to be stable may be compromised by unscrupulous users for personal advantage, resulting in the

breakdown of virtual society. A good example of this is known as *camping* which is a technique of remaining in the same advantagesour virtual location in order to obtain resources and destroy opponents; while not explicitly illegal it makes the game less interesting for other players.

2.2 TYPES OF CHEATING

Taxonomy of cheating methods used in computer games can provide a good starting point for addressing security issues of game design. Prjtchard [342] has proposed six different categories of cheating in online games:

1. **Reflex Augmentation** Using an artificially intelligent computer assistant to perform actions faster and with more precision. For example using an aim-bot in a first person shooter game to quickly and precisely target opponents.

2. **Authoritative Clients** Utilizing hacked clients to send altered commands to other players on the network to deceive about the state of the game.

3. **Information Exposure** Obtaining access to hidden information by compromising client software. For example, using a wall-hack to see your opponents through walls.

4. **Compromised Servers** Changing the game state at the server level to obtain unfair advantage.

5. **Bugs and Design Loopholes** Taking advantage of the poor design of the game software either via security flaws or logical errors in the game model.

6. **Environmental Weaknesses** Abusing operating conditions or hardware configuration of the system's environment.

Yan et al. [465] proposed a broader attack taxonomy incorporating many types of online computer game attacks. In [463] Yan et al. proposed classifying attacks into 15 categories.

A. **Misplaced trust** From the client's side it is possible to modify the game client program, configuration data, or obtain previously unavailable privileges.

B. **Collusion** Combining of forces by multiple players to help each other, share information and work as a team against players not involved in the collusion.

C. **Abuse of procedure or policy** Taking advantage of certain game server policies such as artificially terminating connection to a game server to avoid loosing a game.

D. **Virtual assets** Cheating by acquiring game assets via real money outside of game environment or cheating at real money transactions.

E. **Machine intelligence** Cheating by using artificially intelligent assistant programs, a.k.a. bots to produce superior play. For example asking a world champion chess program to analyze a list of possible moves and representing it as your own.

F. **Client infrastructure** By changing properties of the client infrastructure for example, modifying the graphics driver one can alter the graphics being displayed and thus get access to information like knowing what is on the other side of the brick wall.

G. **Denial of service** Often a server limits the number of login attempts to about three to prevent brute force guessing of passwords. A cheater may purposefully enter incorrect login information for the victim's account to prevent him from logging in to the server. Alternatively a player may be flooded with messages and other interactions preventing participation in a timely manner.

H. **Timing** This cheat involves delaying own action in a real time game until actions of other players are known.

I. **Passwords** A compromised password allows access to another player's account including all the hidden information, virtual resources and ranking scores.

J. **Lack of secrecy** This involves obtaining secret information by observing unencrypted packets as they travel through the network.

K. **Lack of authentication** Obtaining user passwords by setting up a bogus game server.

L. **Design flows** This form of cheating takes advantage of game design mistakes such as exploiting inconsistencies in asset pricing within a virtual environment.

M. **Compromised game servers** A cheater can obtain access to the game host systems and tamper with game server programs.

N. **Internal misuse** An employee of a game server administrator may have privileges for creating virtual assets or super characters which can be sold.

O. Social engineering A method of tricking a player into voluntarily revealing his user name and password, for example by impersonating a request from the game server administration.

Similar classification taxonomies have been proposed by others [288, 114, 311, 425, 59] but most cite Yan et al. [463] as their initial inspiration. The attack types presented above are considered atomic by definition. Complex attacks are comprised of multiple atomic attack techniques used together to achieve multiple goals or to take advantage of a multistage vulnerability. Atomic attacks can also be subdivided into two groups based on the domain of application: game-related and generic network/application security exploits as demonstrated in Table 3.1 [464]:

Type	Label	Cheating Form
Of Special relevance to online games	A	Misplaced Trust
	B	Collusion
	C	Abusing the Game Procedure
	D	Virtual Assets
	E	Exploiting Machine Intelligence
	F	Modifying Client Infrastructure
	H	Timing
Generic	G	Denying Service to Peer Players
	I	Compromising Passwords
	J	Lack of Secrecy
	K	Lack of Authentication
	L	Bug or Design Loophole
	M	Compromised Gamer Servers
	N	Internal Misuse
	O	Social Engineering

Table 3.1: General and game specific attacks (taken from [464])

Yan et al. [464] presented a classification grouped into three categories based on what is exploited, what type of failure can be achieved and who is performing the cheating. From their work it can be seen that cheating is possible mostly due to various security flows and since so many pathways are available to the cheat no single solution is likely to stop all cheating in computer games.

3. SECURITY ISSUES IN ONLINE POKER

While most security issues outlined above (passwords, denial of service, etc.) are valid concerns for online poker participants, many poker specific cheating methods deserve additional overview and analysis [443].

Card eavesdropping Observing the cards of opponents by capturing network traffic is only possible if the information is being transmitted unencrypted which can never happen in a respectable modern online casino. Some information may be gained if a weak or poorly implemented form in encryption is being utilized.

Client hacking As long as the information about the opponents' cards is stored only on the game server and is not transmitted to every client, client hacking is a type of cheating which is not likely to present problems either to other players or to casino operators. Reports exist of people modifying images used by the poker client such as the actual representations of cards. Others have succeeded at hex-editing client software to allow registration of forbidden user names such as those used by casino employees or containing foul language [15].

Exploiting bad randomness Poor design or implementation of a card shuffling algorithm can result in biased card distribution which can be taken advantage of to predict cards before they are revealed. Modern online casinos use independent security companies to verify correctness and security of their software code but in the past this type of problem has been successfully exploited [46].

Escaping In many online casinos if a player gets disconnected because of a network failure or his computer freezes he is considered to be "all-in" for the amount of money he has bet so far. This feature is supposed to protect honest players from being penalized for hardware problems, but is often used by cheaters to avoid loosing additional funds. A cheating player simulates a loss of connection by disconnecting his computer from the network and by doing so avoids committing any more funds to the pot, but is nonetheless in contention for winning portion of the pot.

Profile databases Because players in an online casino have a unique user ID and often play for many months if not years in the same casino it is possible to automate player profiling and to do so in bulk, monitoring all players at the same time. Information about the players' aggressiveness, tendency to bluff, strengths, weaknesses, betting patterns and other statistics is automatically collected and made available for fee. This allows a subscriber to such a service to make educated decisions about strategy against certain players without investing time and funds necessary to learn their playing style. Web sites such as Poker-edge.com and Pokerprophecy.com are two of such services [21, 18].

Collusion (active) A group of players working together attempt to steal pots by raising and re-raising each other to get unsuspecting players with marginal hands to fold. Typically one player has a strong hand while the accomplice is in the pot simply to increase the bets to the point where everyone caught between them folds. Once the contention for the pot is over the weaker of the two hands folds to a raise, and the strong hand gets the pot [380].

Illicit information passing This is the most popular method of online poker cheating. It involves two or more players revealing to each other what cards they are holding. Usually a communications channel independent from the casino such as a phone line or an instant messenger is utilized.

Self collusion Also known as the "Boiler Room" method and "Multi-Accounting", this cheating strategy involves setting up a number of computers in the same location and registering different accounts on each one of them. This allows runnning a poker room where everyone in that room is colluding except for the victim who is cheated out of his money [15].

Player-poker room collusion In this scenario cheaters can manipulate the deck and trap other players into hands where the poker room partner will eventually win. This is accomplished by dealing a very good hand to the unsuspecting player, which as additional community cards become revealed, or even immediately before the flop, is only second best.

Implicit collusion In a tournament settings where, for example, only the top 10 players are paid and there are 11 remaining, implicit collusion involves all players at the table just calling all the way through the river to maximize the likelihood that the short stack will lose by having all hands see the finish. This strategy is never explicitly discussed at the table, but is followed as it gives an advantage to most players.

Chip dumping (tournaments) A group of players who have agreed before the tournament to share profits play against each other very aggressively, with the goal of having one player end up with all the chips, and have the advantage over other players as the chip leader [380].

Excess action hands The poker room deals an excess number of great hands to encourage additional betting action. If the distribution of action hands is not biased it should not hurt individual players in the long run, with the exception of the additional rake being paid to the casino [5].

Rake abuse Casino operator can have a very complicated or dynamic rake structure that reduces players' winnings. As the rake system becomes more complicated it becomes easier for the game operator to add additional fees [5].

Type of Cheating	Cheating Method	Offline	Exploiter			
			Independent		Cooperative	
			Single (account) Player	Casino Operator	Multi (account) Player	Casino-Player
Software Design Flows, Bugs, Abuses	Card eavesdropping	R	P		P	
	Client hacking		P		P	
	Exploiting bad randomness		R		R	
	Escaping		R		R	
	Excess action hands			P		
	Rake abuse			P		
Collusion	Collusion (active)	R			R	P
	Illicit information passing	R			R	P
	Self collusion				R	
	Player-poker room collusion	R				R
	Implicit collusion	R			R	
	Chip dumping (tournaments)	R			R	
Machine Intelligence	Profile databases		R		R	
	Bots		R		R	P
	Bot networks				R	
	Crowd bots			P		

Table 3.2: Taxonomy of cheating in online poker

Bots Artificially intelligent programs designed to play a hand automatically are considered to be a form of cheating by most players and online casinos. While they are currently not very good compared to all but the novice players, they will eventually improve in their performance and present real danger to online poker players of all levels.

Bot networks A number of bots at the same table can be connected to create an information sharking network in which all the bots are actively helping each other to win either by simple information sharing or via active betting. Additionally, an even bigger edge can be obtained if such a bot network has access to an external database of players' profiles.

Crowd bots Some online casinos, particularly newly opened ones, in order to make it seem like they have a large base of regular patrons may employ artificial players to fill in any empty seats at the tables. Depending on quality of such bots it may either be to the advantage or disadvantage of real human players. However, if such bots have access to the information which a regular player would not have access to, such as unrevealed community cards, this might give a huge advantage to the casino.

Table 3.2 shows the taxonomy of cheating methods used in online poker. Each cheating method is grouped according to the type of attack it belongs to, as well as by who is capable of perpetrating such an act. Each attack is marked as either being possible (P) or actually reported (R). A blank means that such cheating method is not possible for a given assailant. "Offline" column is marked if a corresponding cheating method may be used in a regular brick and mortar casino.

4. EXISTING SOLUTIONS

A number of countermeasures have been proposed to combat game security violations, some of them are outlined below [136]:

- **Secure Game Contract** Ensures full synchronization of game state information between all parties of the game and reliable non-repudiatable communication of actions and state changes. Allows for full reconstruction of the game to certify that the game was played properly.

- **Trusted Gaming Infrastructure** Includes gaming operator's security infrastructure, interfaces between different parties, and common elements shared by the network gaming community.

- **Transaction Security** Mechanisms for securing e-commerce transactions, for example, digital signatures and certificates, as well as methods for reliable implementation of distributed transactions.

- **Encryption** Prevents many hacker attacks intended to disrupt or defraud gamers. Protects privacy of players and supports security of e-commerce applications.

- **Regulation, Insurance and Oversight** A third party independent verification of all aspects of game software at the source code level needs to be implemented.

Regulation agencies similar to those in charge of overseeing brick and mortar casinos may need to be set up.

Additional general approaches applicable to the broader field of network security (not just online game security) are suggested by Yan et al. [465]:

- **Built-in cheating detection** An intrusion detection system may be seamlessly incorporated into the game software.

- **Make players security-aware** Players need to be educated about potential security threats for example phishing.

- **Good password practice and management** Users should be educated about what constitutes a secure yet easy to remember password [440].

- **Fair trading** Third parties should be involved in exchange and sale of virtual assets.

- **The bug patching approach** Software flows should be addressed by the developer as they are discovered and patched in a timely manner.

- **An active complain-response channel** A way for players to report bugs and suspected cheating behavior should be provided. A quick response from the game administration is essential to insure players' enthusiasm.

- **Logging and audit trail** Accurate records help to combat insider cheating as well as help in investigation of suspected cheating cases.

- **Post-detection mechanisms** Mitigation of damages from cheaters is an important step in maintaining fairness of the game environment. Cheaters should be punished and victims restored to their original state.

Kimppa et al. [240] proposed the following countermeasures for the acts of cheating encountered in first person shooters, strategy games and role playing games:

Cheat	Countermeasure
Camping (reserving a spot which is ideal for spotting and killing unsuspecting players)	Kicking the player out after a certain time interval.
Non-Stop jumping to make aiming difficult	Preventing sequential jumping over a certain number of jumps at the server level.
Wallhacks (seeing through walls)	Divide map into chunks to hamper the use of the map information.
Reflex augmentation	Kill the process for the well known cheating software
Aim bots	Kill the process for the well known cheating software
Enhanced damage by compromised client	Use checksums
Raw materials which do not belong to the player	Turn beta testing features off
Map revealing software	Don't send unnecessary information to the player
Fake messages from the sever administration	Forbid account names which resemble administrator accounts
Item duplication or creation	Kill the process for the well known cheating software

Table 3.3: Countermeasures for first person shooters, strategy and role playing games (taken from [240])

Since collusion is probably the most frequently used way to cheat in online games we pay particular attention to techniques used to mitigate this form of cheating. Randomized partnering is probably the best known solution to avoid collusion and is most frequently used in online poker tournaments, however it is not helpful in small single table games [462].

Since we are not likely to fully avoid collusion in online poker rooms the next best thing we can do is try to detect it. By evaluating every decision made by the player we can determine if information which is not supposed to be available to the player is being utilized to make a decision. While a single decision may not be sufficient to suspect collusion, a series of optimal actions may provide sufficient proof [413]. Additionally, datamining tools can be used to discover players who always tend to play together or who win more frequently in the presence of particular players. Manually analyzing particular hands with private information about player's hands may also allow us to confirm cases of collusion. This is frequently done after complaints are received from suspicious players at the same table.

5. UNAUTHORIZED GAME BOTS

Artificially Intelligent (AI) programs are quickly becoming a part of our everyday life. Virtual assistants, shopping bots, and smart search engines, to give just some examples, are used daily by millions of people. Such automated intelligent assistants are known as bots, (shortened version of ro**bots)** [452]. In the context of computer games many different bots are known to exist, but all can be classified into one of the three major categories:

- Bots designed to enhance user's intellectual abilities such as chess playing programs which can be consulted to defeat a human opponent who would normally be able to defeat the cheating player.
- Bots aimed at improving the user's physical abilities such as hand-eye coordination. An example would be an aimbot used in first person shooter games to augment the user's reflexes to the point of perfection.
- There is also a large number of bots designed to automate tedious repetitive task such as resource gathering in games like the World of Warcraft.

Bots can also be categorized based on the amount of human participation required:

- **Non-autonomous** Game guides, calculators, statistical tables and other non-interactive sources of help fall into this category. Typically such assistance is not considered to be a form of cheating and so is not the main target of bot detection or prevention research.
- **Simi-autonomous** Bots capable of automatically performing certain set of repetitive tasks, but which require human assistance for at least a part of the game interaction.
- **Fully autonomous** Bots capable of playing the complete game without human intervention. They require no input from human supervisor to either interact with the game software, select between different game options or to terminate play. Some may be equipped with anti-detection capabilities such as ability to simulate simple verbal interaction in the form of a chat.

Two additional types of bots are worth mentioning for the sake of completeness:

- **Bot networks** A number of bots in the same game space can be connected to create an information sharing network in which all bots are actively helping each other to win either by simple information sharing or via active action assistance. Additionally, an even bigger edge can be obtained if such a bot network has access to an external database of player profiles [18, 21].

- **Non-Player Characters (NPC)** Probably the best researched type of bots [94, 319, 144, 242, 315]. They serve as opponents to human players within the games and ideally supposed to closely model intelligent behavior of human players to make the game as interesting and realistic as possible. Current research concentrates on creating human like NPCs with respect to emotion [164], intelligence [256], skills [255, 149] and overall look and feel [79].

Techniques aimed at counteracting bot participation may be used to enforce one of the desirable properties: human presence or human play which are defined by Golle et al. [176, 177]:

Human Presence This property implies that a bot can't play completely unsupervised and a human being is present for at least some interaction with the game software. This somewhat weak condition of human presence precludes numerical explosion of participating bots in a game, by limiting the number of active bots to some function of human beings actually participating in the game. The value of such function depends on a number of bots a single human player may supervise at the same time. The property of human presence guarantees that a human being is investing at least some amount of time into playing the game and so any resource obtained by the bot are not completely free, as time is money.

Human Play Is a much stronger property, which is probably not realistic to achieve and requires that all interaction with the game comes from a human, without any involvement from the bot.

2.1 BOT DETECTION AND COUNTER DETECTION METHODS

Very little literature is published on the subject of game bot detection, perhaps due to the inherent difficulty of the problem. Here we present a short overview of methods known to be used by online casinos and other online game operators. To detect bots the game software may check a number of conditions:

- **Running processes** Which software is running on the system and what network connections are active. This is done to see if well known commercial bots are being run by the user [23].
- **Reaction times** Bots may exhibit a predetermined reaction time as measured from the appearance of stimulus to the making of an action.
- **Duration of play** Bots may be run for unreasonably long periods of time without any breaks. Human beings, and even professional players, are not likely to play for over 12 hours straight.
- **Consistency of behavior** Bots are often utilized to accomplish repetitive tasks within games and so may use exactly the same set of commands to accomplish

their goals, for example always clicking on the exactly the same pixel within the image. This is something a human is unlikely to do or maybe even incapable of doing with high degree of consistency.

- **Network traffic** One of only a few papers to address bot detection in games "Identifying MMORPG Bots: A Traffic Analysis Approach" by Chen et al [113] suggests that a traffic level detection system is possible. Bot generated traffic differs from human generated one with respect to the regularity in the release time of commands, the trend and magnitude of traffic bursts in multiple time scales and the sensitive of interaction to network responsiveness.

If the game software has capacity for inter-player chat engaging the player in a conversation may reveal his true nature. However chat-bots exist and become increasingly better at mimicking an inter-human conversation [371, 126]. They are often incorporated into the game bots as an anti-detection measure. Additional approaches to avoiding bot detection can be clearly seen from analyzing bot detection methods. Bots should be run in a process with a randomly generated name and always for short periods of time, not to exceed a few hours. Bots actions should be randomized both in terms of commands used and spatial and temporal decisions made.

6. BOT PARTICIPATION PREVENTION

With the steady increase in popularity of games and services offered via the Internet the problem of securing such services from automated attacks became apparent. In order to protect limited computational resources against utilization by the growing number of human impersonating bots a methodology in necessary to discriminate between bots and people [338].

In 1950 Alan Turing published his best known paper "Computing Machinery and Intelligence" in which he proposes evaluating abilities of an artificially intelligent machine based on how closely it can mimic human behavior [409]. The test, which is now commonly known as the Turing test is structured as a conversation and can be used to evaluate multiple behavioral parameters, such as agent's knowledge, skills, preferences, and strategies [165]. In essence it is the ultimate multimodal behavioral biometric, which was postulated to make it possible to detect differences between man and machine.

The theoretical platform for an Automated Turing Test (ATT) was developed by Moni Naor in 1996 [320]. The following properties were listed as desirable for the class of problems which can serve as an ATT:

- Many instances of a problem can be automatically generated together with their solutions

- Humans can solve any instance of a problem quickly and with a low error rate. The answer should be easy to provide either by a menu selection or via typing a few characters

- The best known Artificial Intelligence (AI) programs for solving such problems fail a significant percentage of times, despite the full disclosure of how the test problem is generated

- The test problem specification needs to be concise in terms of description and area used to present the test to the user

Since the initial paper by Naor, a great deal of research has been performed in the area, with different researchers frequently inventing new names for the same concept of human/machine disambiguation [55, 362]. In addition to ATT, the developed procedures are known under such names as: Reversed Turing Test (RTT) [121], Human Interactive Proof (HIP) [108], Mandatory Human Participation (MHP) [437], or Completely Automated Public Turing test to tell Computers and Humans Apart (CAPTCHA) [32, 30]. In this chapter we often refer to tests aimed at telling bots and humans apart as CAPTCHAs based on the recent popularity of the term.

As ongoing developments in AI research allow some tests to be broken [111, 312, 25, 314], research continues on developing more secure and user friendly ways of telling machines and humans apart [358, 110, 109, 421, 298, 283]. Such tests are always based on as of yet unsolved problem in AI [31]. Frequent examples include pattern recognition, in particular character recognition [67, 56, 53, 54, 115, 377, 276] or image recognition [116, 275, 132], a number of CAPTCHAs are based on recognition of different biometrics such as faces [306, 356, 357], voice [244, 105] or handwriting [359, 360]. Additionally the following types of tests have been experimented with [183]:

- **Reading** Password displayed as a cluttered image
- **Shape** Identification of complex shapes
- **Spatial** Text image is rendered from a 3D model
- **Quiz** Visual or audio puzzle or trivia question
- **Match** Common theme identification for a set of related images
- **Virtual Reality** Navigation in a 3D world
- **Natural** Uses media files collected from the real world, particularly the web
- **Implicit** Test is incorporated into the web page navigation system [52]

6.1 NON-INTERACTIVE CAPTCHAS

Use of bots, in particular as assistants to a human player, is becoming very popular across multiple game genres from board games such as chess to first person shooters such as Doom. While some argue that bots are like digital steroids for cyber-athletes human-bot teams can be beneficial to the game. Bots can be thought of as a feature not a problem since they enhance level of play and so make the game more interesting. As long as all players have an equal opportunity to enhance their play it should only make the game more competitive, not less interesting for human players.

However, participation of independent bots in most games is undesirable and should be limited to for-bots-only servers run by bot development enthusiasts. Our solution for preventing independent bots from participating in human game networks works particularly well in most card games, such as poker. With our methodology bots become a beneficial feature of the game as they loose money to real human players including the inexperienced beginners, as opposed to emotionless and tireless predators on the weak.

Our work was inspired by the idea of developing implicit human-machine disambiguation procedures and expands on it to provide seamless embedded non-interactive and continuous testing [52]. In particular we developed tests for game environments in which distractive nature of typical tests is particularly detrimental. We are most interested in applying our techniques to card games, such as poker, there bots have been shown to pose the greatest threat to the integrity of the game.

A classical CAPTCHA algorithm can be summarized as follows:

1) Computer generates a test instance

2) Test is shown to the human/bot

3) Human/bot attempts to solve the instance of the test

4) Human/bot reports solution to the computer

5) Computer evaluates the submitted solution

6) Computer reports the result of evaluation to the human/bot and allows or blocks access to a resource based on the result

Figure 3.1 provides a visual representation of the testing procedure.

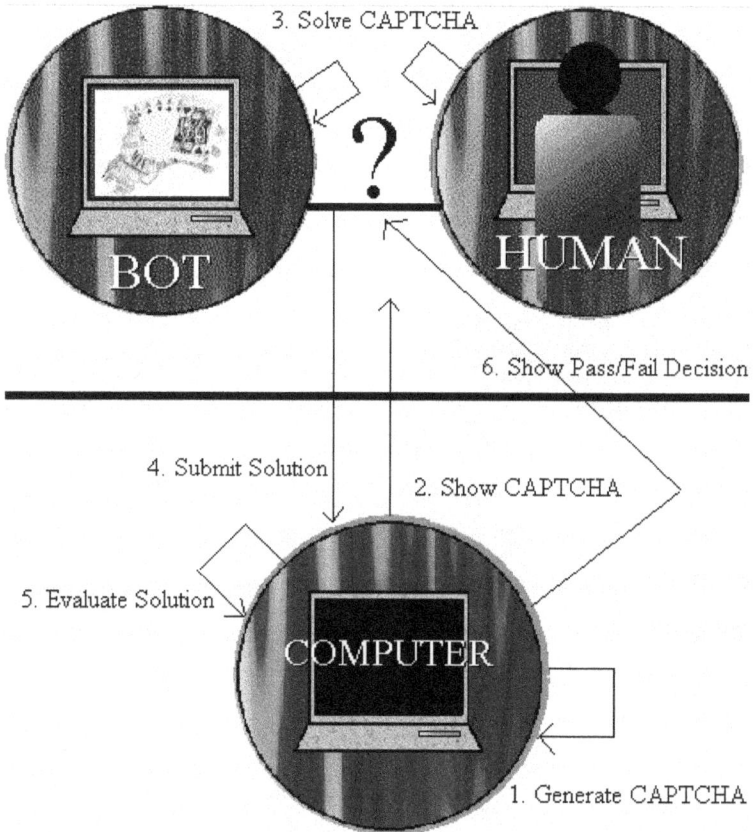

Figure 3.1: Typical human/machine testing algorithm

We propose integrating the testing procedure as a part of the card reading step performed by the player during the game. The identification of the card itself becomes a test which distinguishes bots from legitimate human players. Figure 3.2 demonstrates an embedded test which if properly solved reveals that the card is a King of Hearts. Any well developed text distortion technique employed in traditional CAPTCHA tests can be utilized in our testing procedure.

Figure 3.2: Left: Test embedded in a playing card; Right: Solution – king of hearts

Our proposed embedded non-interactive test works as follows:

1) Computer generates a test instance with solution corresponding to the dealt card
2) Test is shown to the human/bot
3) Human/bot attempts to solve the test
4) Future game decisions of human/bot are shaped by information obtained by solving the test

If the test was solved correctly future decisions of the human/bot can be intelligent as the human/bot is aware of all the necessary information to make decisions. Otherwise the information on which decisions are based is faulty and so decisions are not optimal and the human/bot is essentially acting unintelligently. At no point does a human have to explicitly state his perceived solution for the test reducing the amount of distraction via reduction in necessary interaction. Figure 3.3 demonstrates a number of different test-cards utilized in our experiments. Both private and community cards can be encoded using the proposed methodology [448].

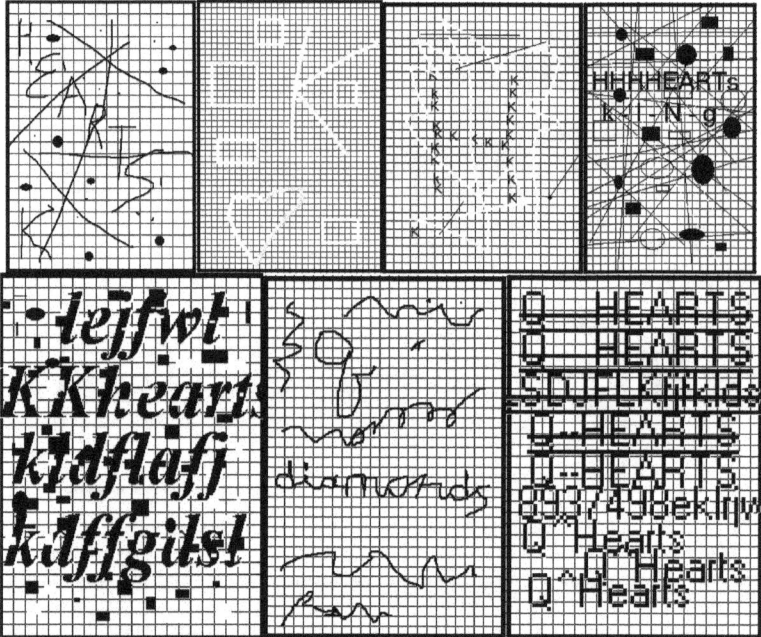

Figure 3.3: Examples of different test-cards

Our methodology has a number of advantages over traditional tests, such as:

1) Less distruction from the task at hand as the test is embedded in the application and is not a separate task requiring human to perform an unrelated activity while taking a forced break from the main application.

2) The bot does not know if the test was passed or failed and so can't learn from its mistakes to improve its performance for future presentations of the test.

3) Bots are not just rejected from obtaining a resource, but are actually punished for trying to access a resource making it less likely that future attempts to obtain the resource will follow.

4) A human who realizes that he has solved the test incorrectly can re-solve it correctly at a future point.

5) Since no solution for a test is provided outsourcing the test becomes not feasible as any answer generated by the solver-for-hire will be accepted but not automatically verifiable as accurate.

Figure 3.4 demonstrates a full ring poker table in an online casino with the player's private cards encoded as tests for telling humans/bots apart. The player has numerous opportunities to solve the test and can even double check his answers to be completely sure. The testing can be made continuous for the duration of the poker hand by making all of the community cards encoded as tests as well.

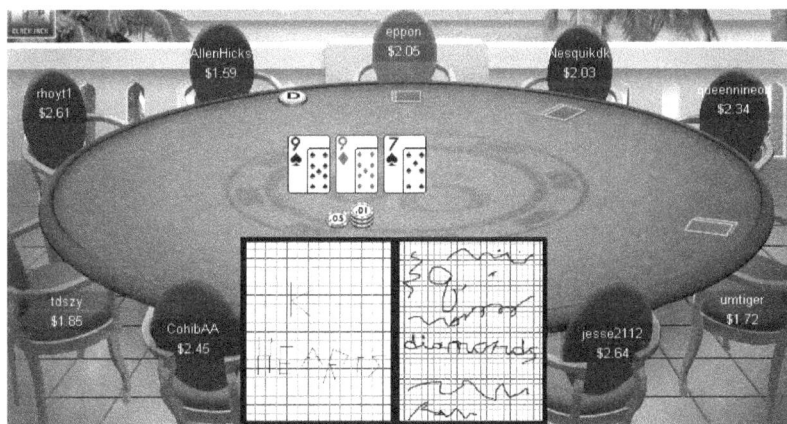

Figure 3.4: Player's private cards with embedded tests

Figure 3.5 demonstrates same poker room interface with the three flop cards encoded to prevent bots from playing or from collecting information about the game. The two still unrevealed community cards (turn and river) will provide additional tests ensuring continuous human participation through the duration of the game.

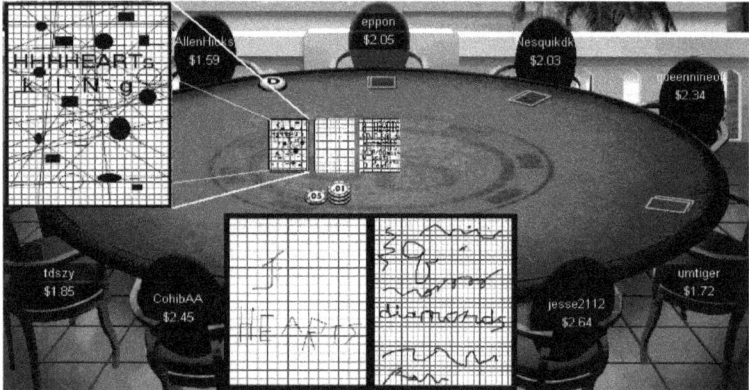

Figure 3.5: Private and community cards with embedded tests

Experimental results obtained with our methodology are encouraging. In a group of volunteers who also happened to be enthusiastic online poker players a very high level of correct card recognition was observed. After initial learning curve of fifteen minutes all of our five volunteers were able to correctly recognize a card in just one second with 99% accuracy. The other one percent corresponded to the most difficult tests and required additional two seconds for correct recognition. As time progressed our volunteers have also reported that the testing procedure started to become less noticeable to the point of being non-obtrusive. Encoding, which our test uses to convert a card's suite and rank to a test format can be accomplished using any well developed CAPTCHA methodology such as text morphing. As a result, performance of human subjects on our tests is equivalent to or exceeds that obtained on a prototype CAPTCHA test because we are dealing with a restricted domain. The prototype CAPTCHA test itself is known to be acceptable for wide groups of human users [358].

7. CONCLUSIONS

With the steady increase in popularity of games and services offered via the Internet the problem of securing such services from automated attacks became apparent. In this chapter we have reviewed cheating methods frequently applied to online computer games alongside approaches used to combat such occurrences. In particular we concentrated on cheating approaches observed at online poker tables and proposed a novel solution for preventing machine intelligence techniques from being used to give an unfair advantage to cheating players.

Use of bots, in particular as assistants to a human player, is becoming very popular across multiple game genres from board games such as chess to first person shooters such as Doom. While some argue that bots are like digital steroids for cyber-athletes human-bot teams can be beneficial to the game. Bots can be thought of as a feature not a problem since they enhance level of play and so make the game more interesting. As long as all players have an equal opportunity to enhance their play it should only make the game more competitive, not less interesting for human players.

However, participation of independent bots in most games is undesirable and should be limited to for-bots-only servers run by bot development enthusiasts. Our solution for preventing independent bots from participating in human game networks works particularly well in most card games. With our methodology bots become a beneficial feature of the game as they lose money to real human players including the inexperienced beginners, as opposed to emotionless and tireless predators on the weak.

In our work we have demonstrated how an embedded non-interactive test can be used to prevent automatic artificially intelligent players from illegally participating in the online game play. Our solution has numerous advantages over traditional tests such as its non-obtrusive nature, continuous verification, and simple non-interactive and outsourcing-proof design. However as with all methods which depend on limitations of current technology, a day will come then artificially intelligent machines will be able to perform at the level indistinguishable from that of their human counterparts.

CHAPTER 4 - BEHAVIORAL BIOMETRICS

"Don't reserve your best behavior for special occasions. You can't have two sets of manners, two social codes – one for those you admire and want to impress, another for those whom you consider unimportant. You must be the same to all people"

Lillian Eichler Watson

Abstract— *In this chapter we survey the state of the art in behavioral biometrics which are based on skills, style, preference, knowledge, motor-skills or strategy used by people while accomplishing different everyday tasks such as driving an automobile, talking on a phone or using a computer. We examine current research and analyze the types of features used to describe behavior. After comparing accuracy rates for verification of users using different behavioral biometrics approaches we address privacy issues which arise with the use of behavioral biometrics.*

1. INTRODUCTION

With the proliferation of computers and of the Internet in our every day lives need for reliable computer security steadily increases. Research in biometric technologies offers one of the most promising approaches to providing user friendly and reliable control methodology for access to computer systems, networks and workplaces [146, 44, 264]. The majority of such research is aimed at studying well established physical biometrics such as fingerprint [100] or iris scans [212]. Behavioral biometrics are usually only briefly mentioned, even in surveys, and only those which are in large part based on muscle control such as keystrokes, gait or signature are well analyzed [83, 211, 410, 139, 355, 382].

Behavioral biometrics provide a number of advantages over traditional biometric technologies. They can be collected non-obtrusively or even without the knowledge of the user. Collection of behavioral data often does not require any special hardware and is so very cost effective. While most behavioral biometrics are not unique enough to provide reliable human identification they have been shown to provide sufficiently high accuracy identity verification.

In accomplishing their everyday tasks human beings employ different strategies, use different styles and apply unique skills and knowledge. One of the defining characteristics of a behavioral biometric is the incorporation of time dimension as a part of the behavioral signature. The measured behavior has a beginning, duration, and an end [8]. Behavioral biometrics researchers attempt to quantify behavioral traits exhibited by users and use resulting feature profiles to successfully verify identity [85]. In this section we present an overview of most established behavioral biometrics.

Behavioral biometrics can be classified into five categories based on the type of information about the user being collected. Category one is made up of authorship based biometrics, which are based on examining a piece of text or a drawing produced by a person. Verification is accomplished by observing style peculiarities typical to the author of the work being examined, such as the used vocabulary, punctuation or brush strokes.

Category two consists of Human Computer Interaction (HCI) based biometrics [449]. In their everyday interaction with computers human beings employ different strategies, use different style and apply unique abilities and knowledge. Researchers attempt to quantify such traits and use resulting feature profiles to successfully verify identity. HCI-based biometrics can be further subdivided into additional categories, first one consisting of human interaction with input devices such as keyboards, computer mice, and haptics which can register inherent, distinctive and consistent muscle actions [4]. The second group consists of HCI-based behavioral biometrics which measure advanced human behavior such as strategy, knowledge or skill exhibited by the user during interaction with different software.

Third group is closely related to the second one and is the set of the indirect HCI-based biometrics which are the events that can be obtained by monitoring user's HCI behaviors indirectly via observable low-level actions of computer software [450]. Those include system call traces [140], audit logs [202], program execution traces [171], registry access [45], storage activity [333], call-stack data analysis [158] and system calls [344, 170]. These low-level events are produced unintentionally by the user during interaction with different software applications while pursuing some, potentially mischievous, high level goals.

Same HCI-based biometrics are sometimes known to different researchers under different names. IDS based on system calls or audit logs are often classified as utilizing program execution traces and those based on call-stack data as based on system calls. The confusion is probably related to the fact that a lot of interdependency exists between different indirect behavioral biometrics and they are frequently used in combinations to improve accuracy of the system being developed. For example system calls and program counter data may be combined in the same behavioral signature or audit logs may contain information about system calls. Also we can't forget that a human being is indirectly behind each one of those reflections of behavior and so a large degree of correlation is to be expected.

Fourth and probably the best researched group of behavioral biometrics relies on motor-skills of the users to accomplish verification [451]. Motor-skill is an ability of a human being to utilize muscles. Muscle movements rely upon the proper functioning of the brain, skeleton, joints, and nervous system and so motor skills indirectly reflect the quality of functioning of such systems, making person verification possible. Most motor skills are learned, not inherited, with disabilities having potential to affect the development of motor skills. We adopt definition for motor-skill based behavioral biometrics, a.k.a. *kinetics,* as those biometrics which are based on innate, unique and stable muscle actions of the user while performing a particular task [4].

Fifth and final category consists of purely behavioral biometrics. Purely behavioral biometrics are those which measure human behavior directly not concentrating on measurements of body parts or intrinsic, inimitable and lasting muscle actions such as the way an individual walks, types or even grips a tool [4]. Human beings utilize different strategies, skills and knowledge during performance of mentally demanding tasks. Purely behavioral biometrics quantify such behavioral traits and make successful identity verification a possibility.

2. BEHAVIORAL BIOMETRICS

Table 4.1 shows behavioral biometrics covered in this chapter classified according to the five categories outlined above. Many of the reviewed biometrics are cross listed in multiple categories due to their dependence on multiple behavioral attributes. In addition enrollment time and verification time (D =days, H=hours, M=Minutes, S=Seconds) of the listed biometrics is provided as well as any hardware required for the collection of the biometric data. Out of all the listed behavioral biometrics only two are believed to be useful not just for person verification but also for reliable large scale person identification, those are: signature/handwriting and speech. Other behavioral biometrics may be used for identification purposes but are not reliable enough to be employed in that capacity in the real world applications.

Classification of the Various Types of Behavioral Biometrics	Authorship	Direct Human Computer Interaction		Indirect Human Computer Interaction	Motor Skill	Purely Behavioral	Properties of Behavioral Biometrics			
		Input Device Interaction Based	Software Interaction Based				Enrollment time	Verification time	Identification	Required Hardware
Audit Logs				•			D	D	N	Computer
Biometric Sketch	•					•	M	S	N	Mouse
Blinking					•		M	S	N	Camera
Call-Stack				•			D	H	N	Computer
Calling Behavior						•	D	D	N	Phone
Car Driving Style						•	H	M	N	Car Sensors
Command Line Lexicon			•			•	H	H	N	Computer
Credit Card Use						•	D	D	N	Credit Card
Dynamic Facial Features					•		M	S	N	Camera
Email Behavior	•		•			•	D	M	N	Computer
Gait/Stride					•		M	S	N	Camera
Game Strategy			•			•	H	H	N	Computer
GUI Interaction				•			D	H	N	Computer
Handgrip					•		M	S	N	Gun Sensors
Haptic		•			•		M	M	N	Haptic
Keystroke Dynamics		•			•		M	S	N	Keyboard
Lip Movement					•		M	S	N	Camera
Mouse Dynamics		•			•		M	S	N	Mouse
Network Traffic				•			D	D	N	Computer
Painting Style	•					•	D	D	N	Scanner
Programming Style	•		•			•	H	H	N	Computer
Registry Access				•			D	H	N	Computer
Signature/Handwriting					•		M	S	Y	Stylus
Storage Activity				•			D	D	N	Computer
System Calls				•			D	H	N	Computer
Tapping					•		M	S	N	Sensor
Text Authorship	•					•	H	M	N	Computer
Voice/Speech/Singing					•		M	S	Y	Microphone

Table 4.1: Classification and properties of behavioral biometrics

Presented below are short overviews of the most researched behavioral biometrics listed in alphabetical order.

Audit Logs

Most modern operating systems keep some records of user activity and program interaction. While such audit trails can be of some interest to behavioral intrusion detection researchers, specialized audit trails specifically designed for security enforcement can be potentially much more powerful. A typical audit log may contain such information as: CPU and I/O usage, number of connections from each location, whether a directory was accessed, a file created, another user ID changed, audit record was modified, amount of activity for the system, network and host [286]. Experimentally it has been shown that collecting audit events is a less intrusive technique than recording system calls [429]. Because an enormous amount of auditing data can be generated overwhelming an intrusion detection system it has been suggested that a random sampling might be a reasonable approach to auditing data [42]. Additional data might be helpful in distinguishing suspicious activity from normal behavior. For example facts about changes in user status, new users being added, terminated users, users on vocations, or changed job assignments might be needed to reduce the number of false positives produced by the IDS [286]. Since so much potentially valuable information can be captured by the audit logs a large number of researchers are attracted to this form of indirect HCI-based biometric [467, 368, 303, 266, 140, 273, 202, 243, 304].

Biometric Sketch

Bromme et al. [86, 34] proposed a biometric sketch authentication method based on sketch recognition and a user's personal knowledge about the drawings content. The system directs a user to create a simple sketch for example of three circles and each user is free to do so in any way he pleases. Because a large number if different combinations exist for combing multiple simple structural shapes sketches of different users are sufficiently unique to provide accurate authentication. The approach measures user's knowledge about the sketch, which is only available to the previously authenticated user. Such features as the sketches location and relative position of different primitives are taken as the profile of the sketch. Similar approaches are tried by Varenhorst [414] with a system called Passdoodles and also by Jermyn et al. [218] with a system called Draw-a-Secret. Finally a V-go Password requests a user to perform simulation of simple actions such as mixing a cocktail using a graphical interface, with the assumption that all users have a personal approach to bartending [348].

Blinking

Westeyn et al. [430, 431] have developed a system for identifying users by analyzing voluntary song-based blink patterns. During the enrollment phase user looks at the system's camera and blinks to the beat of a song he has previously chosen producing a so-called "blinkprint". During verification phase the user's blinking is compared to the database of the stored blinked patterns to determine which song is being blinked and as a result user identification is possible. In addition to the blink pattern itself supplementary features can also be extracted such as: time between blinks, how long the eye is held closed at each blink, and other physical characteristics the eye undergoes while blinking. Based on those additional features it was shown to be feasible to distinguish users blinking the same exact pattern and not just a secretly selected song.

Call-Stack

Feng et al. [157] developed a method for performing anomaly detection using call stack information. The program counter indicates the current execution point of a program; and since each instruction of a program corresponds to a unique program counter this information is useful for intrusion detection. The idea is to extract return addresses from the call stack and generate an abstract execution path between two program execution points. This path is analyzed to decide whether this path is valid based on what has been learned during the normal execution of the program. Return addresses are a particularly good source of information on suspicious behavior. The approach has been shown capable of detecting some attacks that could not be detected by other approaches, while retaining a comparable false positive rate [157]. Additional research into call-stack-based intruder detection has been performed by Giffin et al. [172] and Liu et al. [282].

Calling Behavior

With the proliferation of the mobile cellular phone networks, communication companies are faced with the increasing amount of fraudulent calling activity. In order to automatically detect theft of service many companies are turning to behavioral user profiling with the hopes of detecting unusual calling patterns and be able to stop fraud at an earliest possible time. Typical systems work by generating a user calling profile which consist of use indicators such as: date and time of the call, duration, called ID, called number, cost of call, number of calls to a local destination, number of calls to mobile destinations, number of calls to international destinations and the total statistics about the calls for the day [196]. Grosser et al. [180] have shown that neural networks can be successfully applied to such a feature vector for the purpose of fraud detection. Cahill et al. [95] have addressed ways to improve the selection of the threshold values which are compared with account summaries to see if fraud has taken place. Fawcett et al. [155] developed a rule-learning program to uncover indicators of fraudulent behavior from a large database of customer transactions.

Car driving style

People tend to operate vehicles in very different ways, some drivers are safe and slow others are much more aggressive and often speed and tailgate. As a result, driving behavior can be successfully treated as a behavioral biometric. Erdogan et al. [153, 150, 151] have shown that by analyzing pressure readings from accelerator pedal and brake pedal in kilogram force per square centimeter, vehicle speed in revolutions per minute, and steering angle within the range of -720 to + 720 degrees it is possible to achieve genuine versus impostor driver authentication. Gaussian mixture modeling was used to process the resulting feature vectors, after some initial smoothing and sub-sampling of the driving signal. Similar results were obtained by Igarashi et al. [201] on the same set of multimodal data. Liu et al. [280] in their work on prediction of driver behavior have demonstrated that inclusion of the driver's visual scanning behavior can further enhance accuracy of the driver behavior model. Once fully developed, driver recognition can be used for car personalization, theft prevention, as well as for detection of drunk or sleepy drivers. With so many potential benefits from this technology, research in driver behavior modeling is not solely limited to the biometrics community [328, 251].

Command Line Lexicon

A popular approach to the construction of behavior based intrusion detection systems, is based on profiling the set of commands utilized by the user in the process of interaction with the operating system. A frequent target of such research is UNIX operating system, probably due to it having mostly command line nature. User's differ greatly in their level of familiarity with the command set and all the possible arguments which can be applied to individual commands. Regardless of how well a user knows the set of available commands; most are fairly consistent in their choice of commands used to accomplish a particular task.

A user profile typically consists of a list of used commands together with corresponding frequency counts, and lists of arguments to the commands. Data collection process is often time consuming since as many as 15,000 individual commands need to be collected for the system to achieve high degree of accuracy [365, 297]. Additional information about the secession may also be included in the profile such as the login host and login time, which help to improve accuracy of the user profile as it is likely that users perform different actions on different hosts [133]. Overall, this line of research is extremely popular [469, 293, 259, 260], but recently a shift has been made towards user profiling in a graphical environment such as Windows as most users prefer convenience of a Graphical User Interface (GUI). Typical features extracted from the user's interaction with a windows based machine include: time between windows, time between new windows, number of windows simultaneously open, and number of words in a window title. [175, 233].

Credit Card Use

Data mining techniques are frequently used in detection of credit card fraud. Looking out for unusual transactions, payments to far away geographical locations or simultaneous use of a card at multiple locations can all be signs of a stolen account. Brause et al. [84] have used symbolic and analog number data to detect credit card fraud. Such transaction information as account number, transaction type, credit card type, merchant ID, merchant address, etc. were used in their rule based model. They have also shown that analog data alone can't serve as a satisfying source for detection of fraudulent transactions.

Dynamic Facial Features

Pamudurthy et al. [331] proposed a dynamic approach to face recognition based on dynamic instead of static facial features. They track the motion of skin pores on the face during a facial expression and obtain a vector field that characterizes the deformation of the face. In the training process, two high-resolution images of an individual, one with a neutral expression and the other with a facial expression, like a subtle smile, are taken to obtain the deformation field [291].

Smile recognition research in particular is a subfield of dynamic facial feature recognition currently gaining in prominence [204]. The existing systems rely on probing the characteristic pattern of muscles beneath the skin of the user's face. Two images of a person in quick progression are taken, with subjects smiling for the camera in the second sample. An analysis is later performed of how the skin around the subject's mouth moves between the two images. This movement is controlled by the pattern of muscles under the skin, and is not affected by the presence of make-up or the degree to which the subject smiles [291].

Email Behavior

Email sending behavior is not the same for all individuals. Some people work at night and send dozens of emails to many different addresses; others only check mail in the morning and only correspond with one or two people. All this peculiarities can be used to create a behavioral profile which can serve as a behavioral biometric for an individual. Length of the emails, time of the day the mail is sent, how frequently inbox is emptied and of course the recipients' addresses among other variables can all be combined to create a baseline feature vector for the person's email behavior. Some work in using email behavior modeling was done by Stolfo et al. [393, 394]. They have investigated possibility of detecting virus propagation via email by observing abnormalities in the email sending behavior, such as unusual clique of recipients for the same email. For example sending the same email to your girlfriend and your boss is not an everyday occurrence.

De Vel et al. [415] have applied authorship identification techniques to determine the likely author of an email message. Alongside the typical features used in text authorship identification such as count of function-words and word length frequency distribution authors also used some email specific structural features such as: use of a greeting, farewell acknowledgment, signature, number of attachments, position of re-quoted text within the message body, HTML tag frequency distribution and total number of HTML tags. Overall, almost 200 features are used in the experiment, but some frequently cited features used in text authorship determination are not appropriate in the domain of email messages due to the shorter average size of such communications.

Gait/Stride

Gait is one of the best researched muscle control based biometrics [228, 66, 324], it is a complex spatio-temporal motor-control behavior which allows biometric recognition of individuals at a distance usually from captured video. Gait is subject to significant variations based on changes in person's body weight, waddling during pregnancy, injuries of extremities or of the brain, or due to intoxication [208]. Typical features include: amount of arm swing, rhythm of the walker, bounce, length of steps, vertical distance between head and foot, distance between head and pelvis, maximum distance between the left and right foot [229].

Game Strategy

We have proposed a system for verification of online poker players based on a behavioral profile which represents a statistical model of player's strategy [441, 460, 458]. The profile consists of frequency measures indicating range of cards considered by the player at all stages of the game. It also measures how aggressive the player is via such variables as percentages of re-raised hands. The profile is actually human readable meaning that a poker expert can analyze and understand strategy employed by the player from observing his or her behavioral profile [21]. For example just by knowing the percentage of hands a particular player chooses to play pre-flop it is possible to determine which cards are being played with high degree of accuracy.

Ramon et al. [346] have demonstrated possibility of identifying Go players based on their style of game play. They analyzed a number of Go specific features such as type of opening moves, how early such moves are made and total number of liberties in the formed groups. They also speculate that the decision tree approach they have developed can be applied to other games such as Chess or Checkers.

Jansen et al. [215] report on their research in chess strategy inference from game records. In particular they were able to surmise good estimates of the weights used in the evaluation function of computer chess players and later applied same techniques to human grandmasters. Their approach is aimed at predicting future moves made by the players, but the opponent model created with some additional processing can be utilized for opponent identification or at least verification. This can be achieved by comparing new moves made by the player with predicted ones from models for different players and using the achieved accuracy scores as an indication of which profile models which player.

GUI Interaction

Expanding on the idea of monitoring user's keyboard and mouse activity Garg et al. [170] developed a system for collecting Graphical User Interface (GUI) interaction-based data. Collected data allows for generation of advanced behavioral profiles of the system's users. Such comprehensive data may provide additional information not available form typically analyzed command line data. With proliferation of GUI based systems a shift towards security systems based on GUI interaction data, as opposed to command line data, is a natural progression. Ideally the collected data would include high-level detailed information about the GUI related actions of the user such as: left click on the Start menu, double click on explorer.exe, close Notepad.exe window, etc. Software generated by Garg et al. records all possible low-level user activities on the system in real time, including: system background processes, user run commands, keyboard activity and mouse clicks. All collected information is time stamped and preprocessed to reduce the amount of data actually used for intrusion detection purposes [170].

Handgrip

Developed mostly for gun control applications grip-pattern recognition approach assumes that users hold the gun in a sufficiently unique way to permit user verification to take place. By incorporating a hardware sensor array in the gun's butt Kauffman et al. [232, 417] were able to get resistance measurements in as many as 44 x 44 points which are used in creation of a feature vector. Obtained pressure points are taken as pixels in the pressure pattern image used as input for verification algorithm based on a likelihood-ratio classifier for Gaussian probability densities [232]. Experiments showed that more experienced gun users tended to be more accurately verified as compared to first time subjects.

Haptic

Haptic systems are computer input/output devices which can provide us with information about direction, pressure, force, angle, speed, and position of user's interactions [329, 330]. Because so much information is available about the user's performance a high degree of accuracy can be expected from a haptic based biometrics system. Orozco et al. [329, 330] have created a simple haptic application built on an elastic membrane surface in which the user is required to navigate a stylus through the maze. The maze has gummy walls and a stretchy floor. The application collects data about the ability of the user to navigate the maze, such as reaction time to release from sticky wall, the route, the velocity, and the pressure applied to the floor. The individual user profiles are made up of such information as 3D world location of the pen, average speed, mean velocity, mean standard deviation, navigation style, angular turns and rounded turns.

In a separate experiment Orozco et al. [401] implement a virtual mobile phone application where the user interacts through a haptic pen to simulate making a phone call via a touch pad. The keystroke duration, pen's position, and exerted force are used as the raw features collected for user profiling.

Keystroke Dynamics

Typing patterns are characteristic to each person, some people are experienced typists utilizing the touch-typing method, and others utilize the hunt-and-peck approach which uses only two fingers. Those differences make verification of people based on their typing patterns a proven possibility, some reports suggest identification is also possible [203]. For verification a small typing sample such as the input of user's password is sufficient, but for recognition a large amount of keystroke data is needed and identification is based on comparisons with the profiles of all other existing users already in the system.

Keystroke features are based on time durations between the keystrokes, inter-key strokes and dwell times, which is the time a key is pressed down, overall typing speed, frequency of errors (use of backspace), use of numpad, order in which user presses shift key to get capital letters and possibly the force with which keys are hit for specially equipped keyboards [203, 208]. Keystroke dynamics is probably the most researched type of HCI-based biometric [310, 68], with novel research taking place in different languages [181], for long text samples, [130, 61] and for email authorship identification [182].

In a similar fashion Bella et al. [65] have studied finger movements of skilled piano players. They have recorded finger motion from skilled pianists while playing a musical keyboard. Pianists' finger motion and speed with which keys are struck was analyzed using functional data analysis methods. Movement velocity and acceleration were consistent for the participants and in multiple musical contexts. Accurate pianists' classification was achieved by training a neural network classifier using velocity/acceleration trajectories preceding key presses.

Lip Movement

This approach originally based on the visual speech reading technology attempts to generate a model representing lip dynamics produced by a person during speech. User verification is based on how close the generated model fits observed lip movement. Such models are typically constructed around spatio-temporal lip features. First the lip region needs to be isolated from the video feed, and then significant features of lip contours are extracted typically from edges and gradients. Lip features include: the mouth opening or closing, skin around the lips, mouth width, upper/lower lip width, lip opening height/width, distance between horizontal lip line and upper lip [373, 91]. Typically lip dynamics are utilized as a part of a multimodal biometric system, usually combined with speaker recognition based authentication [284, 422, 294, 222], but standalone usage is also possible [307].

Mouse Dynamics

By monitoring all mouse actions produced by the user during interaction with the Graphical User Interface (GUI), a unique profile can be generated which can be used for user re-authentication [344]. Mouse actions of interest include general movement, drag and drop, point and click, and stillness. From those a set of features can be extracted for example average speed against the distance traveled, and average speed against the movement direction [29, 28]. Pusara et al. [344] describe a feature extraction approach in which they split the mouse event data into mouse wheel movements, clicks, menu and toolbar clicks. Click data is further subdivided into single and double click data.

Gamboa et al. [167, 168] have tried to improve accuracy of mouse-dynamics-based biometrics by restricting the domain of data collection to an online game instead of a more general GUI environment. As a result applicability of their results is somewhat restricted and the methodology is more intrusive to the user. The system requires around 10-15 minutes of devoted game play instead of seamless data collection during the normal to the user human computer interaction. As far as the extracted features, x and y coordinates of the mouse, horizontal velocity, vertical velocity, tangential velocity, tangential acceleration, tangential jerk and angular velocity are utilized with respect to the mouse strokes to create a unique user profile.

Network Traffic

Network level intrusion detection is somewhat different from other types of intrusion detection as the monitored activity originates outside the system being protected. With the increase in popularity of Internet and other networks an intruder no longer has to have physical access to the system he is trying to penetrate. This means that the network dataflow arriving on different system ports and encoded using different protocols needs to be processed and reviewed. IDS based on network traffic analyze various packet attributes such as: IP protocol-type values, packet size, server port numbers, source and destination IP prefixes, Time-To-Live values, IP/TCP header length, incorrect IP/TCP/UDP checksums, and TCP flag patterns. During the baseline profiling period the number of packets with each attribute value is counted and taken as normal behavior [239]. Any deviation from the normal baseline profile may set an alert flag informing network administrator that an attack is taking place. Many behavior based security systems have been developed based on the concept of network level attack detection [376, 473, 383, 326, 325, 327] and the general area of network traffic analysis is highly applicable for improved network and network application design [281, 396].

Painting Style

Just like authorship of literary works can be attributed based on the writers style, so can the works of art be accredited based on the style of the drawing. In particular the subtle pen and brush strokes characteristic of a particular painter can be profiled. Lyu et al. [289] developed a technique for performing a multi-scale, multi-orientation painting scan decomposition. This decomposition changes the basis from functions maximally localized in space to one in which the basis functions are also localized in orientation and scale. By constructing a compact model of the statistics from such a function it is possible to detect consistencies or inconsistencies between paintings and drawings supposedly produced by the same author.

Programming Style

With the increasing number of viruses, worms, and Trojan horses it is often useful in a forensic investigation to be able to identify an author of such malware programs based on the analysis of the source code. It is also valuable for the purposes of software debugging and maintenance to know who the original author of a certain code fragment was. Spafford et al. [386] have analyzed a number of features potentially useful for the identification of software authorship. In case only the executable code is available for analysis, data structures and applied algorithms can be profiled as well as any remaining compiler and system information, observed programming skill level, knowledge of the operating system and choice of the system calls. Additionally use of predefined functions and provisions for error handling are not the same for different programmers.

In case the original source files are available a large number of additional identifying features become accessible such as: chosen programming language, code formatting style, type of code editor, special macros, style of comments, variable names, spelling and grammar, use of language features such as choice of loop structures, the ratio of global to local variables, temporary coding structures, and finally types of mistakes observable in the code. Software metrics such as number of lines of code per function, comment-to-code ratio and function complexity may also be introduced [386]. Similar code features are discussed by Gray et al. [178] and in Grantzeskou et al. [163].

Registry Access

Apap et al. [45] proposed a new type of host-based security approach they call Registry Anomaly Detection (RAD) that monitors access to the Windows registry in real time and detects the actions of malicious software. Windows registry stores information about hardware installed on the system, which ports are used, user profiles, policies, user names, passwords and configuration settings for programs. Most programs access a certain set of registry keys during normal operation. Similarly most users use only a certain subset of programs available on the machine. This results in a high degree of regularity in registry interaction during the normal operation of the system. However, malicious software may substantially deviate from this regular activity and can be detected. Many attacks involve starting programs which have rarely been used in the past or changing keys that have never been changed before. If a RAD system is trained on clean data, then these kinds of registry operations will appear abnormal to the system and result in issue of an alert [45].

Signature/Handwriting

Signature verification is a widely accepted methodology for confirming identity [207, 318, 192, 269]. Two distinct approaches to signature verification are traditionally recognized based on the data collection approach, they are: on-line and off-line signature verification also known as static and dynamic approaches [351]. In the off-line signature verification the image of the signature is obtained using a scanning device, possibly some time after the signing took place. With on-line signature verification special hardware is used to capture dynamics of the signature, typically pressure sensitive pens in combination with digitizing tablets are utilized. Because on-line data acquisition methodology obtains features not available in the off-line mode, dynamic signature verification is more reliable [316].

With on-line signature verification in addition to the trajectory coordinates of the signature, other features like pressure at pen tip, acceleration and pen-tilt can be collected. In general signature related features can be classified into two groups: global and local. Global features include: signing speed, signature bounding box, Fourier descriptors of the signature's trajectory, number of strokes, and signing flow. Local features describe specific sample point in the signature and relationship between such points, for example distance and curvature change between two successive points may be analyzed as well as x and y offsets relative to the first point on the signature trajectory, and critical points of the signature trajectory [316, 336].

Signature-based user verification is a particular type of general handwriting based biometric authentication. Unlike with signatures, handwriting-based user verification/recognition is content independent, which makes the process somewhat more complicated [58, 345, 57]. Each person's handwriting is seen as having a specific texture. The spatial frequency and orientation contents represent the features of each texture [474]. Since handwriting provides a much more substantial biometric sample in comparison to signatures respective verification accuracy can be much greater.

Soft Behavioral Biometrics

Jain et al. [209, 210] define soft biometrics as: "...traits as characteristics that provide some information about the individual, but lack the distinctiveness and permanence to sufficiently differentiate any two individuals". They further state that soft biometric traits can either be continuous such as height or weight or discrete such as gender or ethnicity. We propose expending the definition to include soft behavioral biometrics, which also can be grouped into continuous and discrete types. Continuous soft behavioral biometric traits include measurements produced by various standardized tests, some of the most popular such tests are IQ test for intelligence, and verbal sections of SAT, GRE, GMAT for language abilities. Discrete soft behavioral biometrics are skills which a particular person either has or does not have. Examples of such include ability to speak a particular foreign language, knowledge of how to fly a plane, ride a motorcycle, etc.

While such soft behavioral biometrics are not sufficient for identification or verification of individuals they can be combined with other biometric approaches to increase system accuracy. They can also be used in certain situations to reject individual's verification claim. For example in a case of academic cheating a significantly fluctuating score on a repeatedly taken standardized test can be used to suspect that not the same person answered all the questions on a given test [206].

Storage Activity

Many actions of intruders became visible at the storage level interface. Manipulation of system utilities (to add backdoors), tampering with audit logs (to destroy evidence), resetting of attributes (to hide changes) and addition of suspicious content (known virus) all show up as the changes in the storage layer of the system. A storage-based security system analyzes all requests received by the storage server and can issue alerts about suspicious activity to the system administrator. Additionally it can slow down the suspected intruder's storage access or isolate intruder via a forking of version trees to a sandbox. Storage-based security approach has the advantage of being independent from the client's operating system and so can continue working after the initial compromise, unlike host-based security systems which can be disabled by the intruder [333]. Research using storage activity is fast gaining in popularity with intrusions being detected at the block storage level [391], in Storage Area Network (SAN) environments [60], object-based storage devices [472], workstation disk drives [179] and in the context of the overall intrusion detection [391].

System Calls

A system call is the method used by a program to request service from the operating system, or more particularly, the operating system kernel. System calls use a special instruction which causes the processor to transfer control to a more privileged code segment. Intruder detection can be achieved by comparing an application's run-time system calls with a pre-defined normal system call behavior model. The assumption is that as long as the intruder can't make arbitrary system calls, it is unlikely that he can achieve his desired malicious goals [257]. Following the original work of Forest et al. [198, 423] a number of researchers have pursuit development of security systems based on analyzing system call sequences [257, 172, 322, 292, 420, 171]. Typically a model of normal system call behavior is learned during the training phase which is a baseline-state assumed to be free of attacks [69], alternative approaches use static analysis of the source code or binary code [172]. A number of representation schemas for the behavioral model have been proposed, including strings [423, 429], finite state automata and push down automata [157, 172].

Tapping

Henderson et al. [191, 190] have studied the idea of tapping recognition, based on the idea that you are able to recognize who is knocking on your door. They concentrated on the waveform properties of the pulses which result from tapping the polymer thick-film sensor on a smart card. Produced pressure pulses are further processed to extract useful features such as: pulse height, pulse duration, and the duration of the first inter-pulse interval. The recognition algorithm utilized in this research has been initially developed for processing of keyboard dynamics, which is a somewhat similar technology of recognizing tapping with respect to keyboard keys.

Text Authorship

Email and source code authorship identification represent application and improvement of techniques developed in a broader field of text authorship determination. Written text and spoken word once transcribed can be analyzed in terms of vocabulary and style to determine its authorship. In order to do so a linguistic profile needs to be established. Many linguistic features can be profiled such as: vocabulary, lexical patterns, syntax, semantics, pragmatics, information content or item distribution through a text [184]. Stematatos et al. [389] in their analysis of modern Greek texts proposed using such text descriptors as: sentence count, word count, punctuation mark count, noun phrase count, word included in noun phrase count prepositional phrase count, word included in prepositional phrase count and keyword count. Overall area of authorship attribution is very promising with a lot of ongoing research [224, 245, 246].

Voice/Speech/Singing

Speaker identification is one of the best researched biometric technologies [120, 363, 96]. Verification is based on information about the speaker's anatomical structure conveyed in amplitude spectrum, with the location and size of spectral peaks related to the vocal tract shape and the pitch striations related to the glottal source of the user [229]. Speaker identification systems can be classified based on the freedom of what is spoken [347]:

- **Fixed text:** The speaker says a particular word selected at enrollment.

- **Text dependent:** The speaker is prompted by the system to say a particular phrase.

- **Text independent:** The speaker is free to say anything he wants, verification accuracy typically improves with larger amount of spoken text.

Feature extraction is applied to the normalized amplitude of the input signal which is further decomposed into several band-pass frequency channels. A frequently extracted feature is a logarithm of the Fourier Transform of the voice signal in each band along with pitch, tone, cadence, and shape of the larynx [208]. Accuracy of voice based biometrics systems can be increased by inclusion of visual speech (lip dynamics) [284, 422, 294, 222] and incorporation of soft behavioral biometrics such as accent [141, 278].

Recently some research has been aimed at expanding the developed technology to singer recognition for the purposes of music database management [402] and to laughter recognition. Currently, the laughter-recognition software is rather crude and cannot accurately distinguish between different people [291, 204].

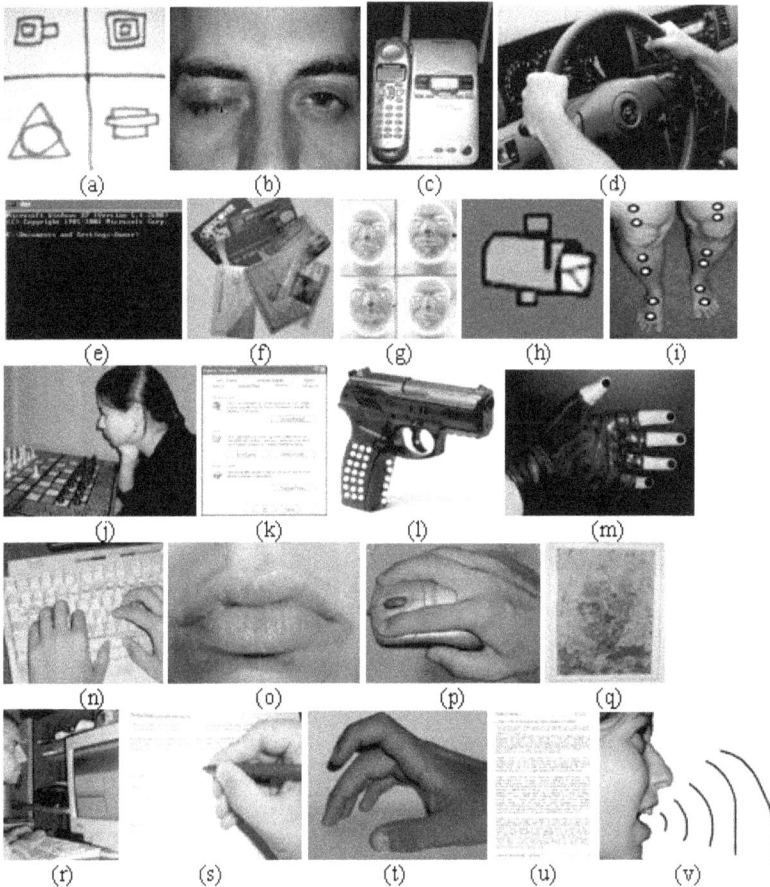

Figure 4.1: Examples of Behavioral Biometrics: a) Biometric Sketch, b) Blinking, c) Calling, d) Car Driving, e) Command Line Lexicon, f) Credit Card Use, g) Dynamic Facial Features, h) Email, i) Gait, j) Game Strategy, k) GUI Interaction, l) Handgrip, m) Haptic, n) Keystrokes, o) Lip Movement, p) Mouse Dynamics, q) Painting Style, r) Programming Style, s) Signature, t) Tapping, u) Text Authorship, v) Voice.

3. ARCHITECTURE OF BEHAVIORAL BIOMETRIC SYSTEMS

In this section we describe a generalized algorithm for behavioral biometrics, which can be applied to any type of human activity. The first step is to break up the behavior in question into a number of atomic operations each one corresponding to a single decision. Ideally all possible operations should be considered, but in a case of behavior with a very large repertoire of possible operations a large subset of most frequent operations might be sufficient.

User's behavior should be observed and a frequency count for the occurrence of the atomic operations should be produced. The resulting frequency counts form a feature vector which is used to verify or reject the user based on the similarity score produced by a similarity function. An experimentally determined threshold serves as a decision boundary for separating legitimate users from intruders. In case user identification is attempted a neural network or a decision tree approach might be used to select the best matching user from the database of existing templates. Below we outline the proposed generalized algorithm:

1 Pick a behavior
2 Break up behavior into component actions
3 Determine frequencies of component actions for each user
4 Combine results into a feature vector profile
5 Apply similarity measure function to the stored template and current behavior
6 Experimentally determine a threshold value
7 Verify or reject user based on the similarity score comparison to the threshold value

Step 5 in the above algorithm is not trivial and over the years a lot of research has gone into understanding what makes a good similarity measure function for different biometric systems. A good similarity measure takes into account statistical characteristics of the data distribution assuming enough data is available to determine such properties [264].

4. COMPARISON AND ANALYSIS OF BEHAVIORAL BIOMETRICS

All of the presented behavioral biometrics share a number of characteristics and so can be analyzed as a group using seven properties of good biometrics presented by Jain et al. [208, 212].

- **Universality** Behavioral biometrics are dependent on specific abilities possessed by different people to a different degree or not at all and so in a general population universality of behavioral biometrics is very low. But since behavioral biometrics are only applied in a specific domain, the actual universality of behavioral biometrics is a 100%.

- **Uniqueness** Since only a small set of different approaches to performing any task exists uniqueness of behavioral biometrics is relatively low. Number of existing writing styles, different game strategies and varying preferences are only sufficient for user verification not identification unless the set of users is extremely small [26].

- **Permanence** Behavioral biometrics exhibit a low degree of permanence as they measure behavior which changes with time as person learns advanced techniques and faster ways of accomplishing tasks. However, this problem of concept drift is addressed in the behavior based intrusion detection research and systems are developed capable of adjusting to the changing behavior of the users [247, 405, 367].

- **Collectability** Collecting behavioral biometrics is relatively easy and unobtrusive to the user. In some instances the user may not even be aware that data collection is taking place. The process of data collection is fully automated and is very low cost.

- **Performance** The identification accuracy of most behavioral biometrics is low particularly as the number of users in the database becomes large. However verification accuracy is very good for some behavioral biometrics.

- **Acceptability** Since behavioral biometrics can be collected without user participation they enjoy a high degree of acceptability, but might be objected to for ethical or privacy reasons.

- **Circumvention** It is relatively difficult to get around behavioral biometric systems as it requires intimate knowledge of someone else's behavior, but once such knowledge is available fabrication might be very straightforward [366]. This is why it is extremely important to keep the collected behavioral profiles securely encrypted.

All behavioral biometrics essentially measure human actions which result from specific to every human skills, style, preference, knowledge, motor-skills or strategy. Table 4.2 summarizes what precisely is being measured by different behavioral biometrics as well as lists some of the most frequently used features for each type of behavior. Indirect HCI-based biometrics are not included as they have no meaning independent of the direct human computer interaction which causes them. Motor-skill based biometrics measure innate, unique and stable muscle actions of users performing a particular task. Table 4.3 outlines which muscle groups are responsible for a particular motor-skill as well as lists some of the most frequently used features for each muscle control based biometric approach.

Behavioral Biometric	Measures	Features
Biometric Sketch	Knowledge	location and relative position of different primitives
Calling Behavior	Preferences	date and time of the call, duration, called ID, called number, cost of call, number of calls to a local destination, number of calls to mobile destinations, number of calls to international destinations
Car driving style	Skill	pressure from accelerator pedal and brake pedal, vehicle speed, steering angle
Command Line Lexicon	Technical Vocabulary	used commands together with corresponding frequency counts, and lists of arguments to the commands
Credit Card Use	Preferences	account number, transaction type, credit card type, merchant ID, merchant address
Email Behavior	Style	length of the emails, time of the day the mail is sent, how frequently inbox is emptied, the recipients' addresses
Game Strategy	Strategy/Skill	count of hands folded, checked, called, raised, check-raised, re-raised, and times player went all-in
Haptic	Style	3D world location of the pen, average speed, mean velocity, mean standard deviation, navigation style, angular turns and rounded turns
Keystroke Dynamics	Skill	time durations between the keystrokes, inter-key strokes and dwell times, which is the time a key is pressed down, overall typing speed, frequency of errors (use of backspace), use of numpad, order in which user presses shift key to get capital letters
Mouse Dynamics	Style	x and y coordinates of the mouse, horizontal velocity, vertical velocity, tangential velocity, tangential acceleration, tangential jerk and angular velocity
Painting Style	Style	subtle pen and brush strokes characteristic
Programming Style	Skill, Style, Preferences	chosen programming language, code formatting style, type of code editor, special macros, comment style, variable names, spelling and grammar, language features, the ratio of global to local variables, temporary coding structures, errors
Soft Behavioral Biometrics	Intelligence, Vocabulary, Skills	word knowledge, generalization ability, mathematical skill
Text Authorship	Vocabulary	sentence count, word count, punctuation mark count, noun phrase count, word included in noun phrase count prepositional phrase count, word included in prepositional phrase count and keyword count

Table 4.2 Summary of behavioral biometrics with corresponding traits and features

Motor Skill	Muscles Involved	Extracted Features
Blinking	orbicularis oculi, corrugator supercilii, depressor supercilii	time between blinks, how long the eye is held closed at each blink, physical characteristics the eye undergoes
Dynamic Facial Features	levator labii superioris, levator anguli oris zygomaticus major, zygomaticus minor, mentalis, depressor labii inferioris, depressor anguli oris, buccinator, orbicularis oris	motion of skin pores on the face
Gait/Stride	tibialis anterior, extensor hallucis longus, extensor digitorum longus, peroneus tertius, extensor digitorum brevis, extensor hallucis brevis, gastrocnemius, soleus, plantaris, popliteus, flexor hallucis longus flexor digitorum longus	amount of arm swing, rhythm of the walker, bounce, length of steps, vertical distance between head and foot, distance between head and pelvis, maximum distance between the left and right foot
Handgrip	abductor pollicis brevis, opponens pollicis, flexor pollicis brevis, adductor pollicis, palmaris brevis, abductor minimi digiti, flexor brevis minimi digiti	resistance measurements in multiple points
Haptic	abductor pollicis brevis, opponens pollicis,l flexor pollicis brevis, adductor pollicis, palmaris brevis, abductor minimi digiti,l flexor brevis minimi digiti, opponens digiti minimi, lumbrical, dorsal interossei	3D world location of the pen, average speed, mean velocity, mean standard deviation, navigation style, angular turns and rounded turns
Keystroke Dynamics	abductor pollicis brevis, opponens pollicis, flexor pollicis brevis, adductor pollicis, palmaris brevis, abductor minimi digiti, flexor brevis minimi digiti, opponens digiti minimi, lumbrical, dorsal interossei, palmar interossei	time durations between the keystrokes, inter-key strokes and dwell times, which is the time a key is pressed down, overall typing speed, frequency of errors (use of backspace), use of numpad, order in which user presses shift key to get capital letters
Lip Movement	levator palpebrae superiorisj, levator anguli oris, mentalis, depressor labii inferioris, depressor anguli oris, buccinator	mouth width, upper/lower lip width, lip opening height/width, distance between horizontal lip line and upper lip
Mouse Dynamics	abductor pollicis brevis, opponens pollicis, flexor pollicis brevis, adductor pollicis, palmaris brevis, abductor minimi digiti, flexor brevis minimi digiti, opponens digiti minimi, lumbrical, dorsal interossei, palmar interossei	x and y coordinates of the mouse, horizontal velocity, vertical velocity, tangential velocity, tangential acceleration, tangential jerk and angular velocity
Signature/ Handwriting	abductor pollicis brevis, opponens pollicis, flexor pollicis brevis, adductor pollicis, palmaris brevis, abductor minimi digiti, flexor brevis minimi digiti, opponens digiti minimi, lumbrical, dorsal interossei, palmar interossei	coordinates of the signature, pressure at pen tip, acceleration and pen-tilt, signing speed, signature bounding box, Fourier descriptors of the signature's trajectory, number of strokes, and signing flow
Tapping	abductor pollicis brevis, opponens pollicis, flexor pollicis brevis, adductor pollicis, palmaris brevis, abductor minimi digiti	pulse height, pulse duration, and the duration of the first inter-pulse interval
Voice/ Speech	cricothyroid, posterior ricoarytenoid, lateral cricoarytenoid, arytenoid, thyroarytenoid	logarithm of the Fourier transform of the voice signal in each band along with pitch, tone, cadence

Table 4.3: Summary of motor-skill biometrics with respective muscles and features [390]

While many behavioral biometrics are still in their infancy some very promising research has already been done. The results obtained justify feasibility of using behavior for verification of individuals and further research in this direction is likely to improve accuracy of such systems.

Table 4.4 summarizes obtained accuracy ranges for the set of direct behavioral biometrics for which such data is available.

Table 4.5 reports detection rates and error rates for indirect human computer interaction based behavioral biometrics.

Behavioral Biometric	Publication	Recognition/ Detection Rate	FAR	FRR	EER
Biometric Sketch	Bromme 2003 [86]				7.2%
Blinking	Westeyn 2004 [431]	82.02%			
Calling Behavior	Fawcett 1997 [155]	92.5%			
Car driving style	Erdogan 2005 [150]	88.25%			4.0%
Command Line Lexicon	Marin 2001 [293]	74.4%		33.5%	
Credit Card Use	Brause 1999 [84]	99.995%		20%	
Email Behavior	de Vel 2001 [415]	90.5%			
Gait/Stride	Kale 2004 [228]	90%			
Game Strategy	Yampolskiy 2007 [458]				7.0%
Handgrip	Veldhuis 2004 [417]				1.8%
Haptic	Orozco 2006 [330]		25%		22.3%
Keystroke Dynamics	Bergadano 2002 [68]		0.01%	4%	
Lip Movement	Mok 2004 [307]				2.17%
Mouse Dynamics	Pusara 2004 [344]		0.43%	1.75%	
Programming Style	Frantzeskou 2004 [163]	73%			
Signature Handwriting	Jain 2002 [207] Zhu 2000 [474]	95.7%	1.6%	2.8%	
Tapping	Henderson 2001 [191]				2.3%
Text Authorship	Halteren 2004 [184]		0.2%	0.0%	
Voice/Speech Singing	Colombi 1996 [123] Tsai 2006 [403]				0.28% 29.6%

Table 4.4: Recognition, verification and error rates of behavioral biometrics

Type of Indirect Biometric	Publication	Detection Rate	False Positive Rate
Audit Logs	Lee 1999 [266]	93%	8%
Call-Stack	Feng 2003 [158]	-	1%
GUI Interaction	Garg 2006 [170]	96.15%	3.85%
Network Traffic	Zhang 2003 [473]	96.2%	.0393%
Registry Access	Apap 2001 [45]	86.9%	3.8%
Storage Activity	Stanton 2005 [391]	97%	4%
System Calls	Ghosh 1999 [171]	86.4%	4.3%

Table 4.5: Detection and false positive rates for indirect behavioral biometrics

An unintended property of behavioral profiles is that they might contain information which may be of interest to third parties which have potential to discriminate against individuals based on such information. As a consequence intentionally revealing or obtaining somebody else's behavioral profile for the purposes other than verification is highly unethical. Examples of private information which might be revealed by some behavioral profiles follow:

- **Calling Behavior** Calling data is a particularly sensitive subject since it might reveal signs of infidelity or interest in non-traditional adult entertainment.
- **Car driving style** Car insurance companies may be interested to know if a driver frequently speeds and is an overall aggressive driver in order to charge an increased coverage rate or to deny coverage all together.
- **Command Line Lexicon** Information about proficiency with the commands might be used by an employer to decide if you are sufficiently qualified for a job involving computer interaction.
- **Credit Card Use** Credit card data reveals information about what items you frequently purchase and in what locations you can be found violating your expectation of privacy. For example an employer might be interested to know if an employee buys a case of beer every day indicating a problem with alcoholism.
- **Email Behavior** An employer would be interested to know if employees send out personal emails during office hours.
- **Game Strategy** If information about game strategy is obtained by the player's opponents it might be analyzed to find weaknesses in player's game and as a result gives an unfair advantage to the opponents.
- **Programming Style** Software metric obtained from analysis of code may indicate a poorly performing coder and as a result jeopardize the person's employment.

Additionally, any of the motor-skill based biometrics may reveal a physical handicap of a person and so result in potential discrimination. Such biometrics as voice can reveal emotions, and the face images may reveal information about emotions and health [127]. Because behavioral biometric indirectly measure our thoughts and personal traits any data collected in the process of generation of a behavioral profile needs to be safely stored in an encrypted form.

5. CONCLUSIONS

Reliable security to a large degree depends on development of biometric technology in general and behavioral biometrics in particular. This affordable and non-intrusive way of verifying user's identity holds a lot of potential to develop secure and user friendly systems, networks and workplaces. As long as the issues of privacy are sufficiently addressed by the developers of behavior based security systems commercial potential of development in this area is very substantial [219, 364].

In this survey we have presented the most popular behavioral biometrics but any human behavior can be used as a basis for personal profiling and for subsequent verification. Potential areas of future research include profiling of shopping behavior [341], web browsing [274, 166, 174], or even TV preferences [22]. Behavioral biometrics are particularly well suited for verification of users which interact with computers, cell phones, smart cars, or points of sale terminals. As the number of electronic appliances used in homes and offices increases so does the potential for utilization of this novel and promising technology. Future research should be directed at increasing overall accuracy of such systems, for example by looking into possibility of developing multimodal behavioral biometrics, as people often engage in multiple behaviors at the same time., for example, talking on a cell phone while driving or using keyboard and mouse at the same time [213, 131, 200].

CHAPTER 5 - COMPARISON OF PASSTEXT, PASSART AND PASSMAP FOR USER AUTHENTICATION

"If life doesn't offer a game worth playing, then invent a new one"

Anthony J. D'Angelo

Abstract—*Network security partially depends on reliable user authentication; unfortunately currently used passwords are not completely secure. One of the main problems with passwords is that very good passwords are hard to remember and the ones which are easy to remember are too short or simple to be secure. We have designed a number of authentication schemas, which are easy to remember and can be relatively quickly provided to the system, while at the same time remain impossible to break with brute force alone. In this chapter we have compared the size of password spaces and how easy they are to remember for many popular alphanumeric and graphical authentication schemas against the approaches developed by us, namely PassText, PassArt and PassMap.*

1. INTRODUCTION

As the computer technology keeps growing in importance in our every day lives, it becomes increasingly important to provide safe and secure ways to authenticate users of different systems, to allow people access to the information, networks and decision making modules. The first and most important step in network and computer security is reliable user authentication. For decades simple passwords were sufficient for insuring that only authorized individuals had access to privileged resources and information. As computers became more computationally powerful, brute force attacks on the previously unprecedented scale became possible. Combined with the tendency of users to create simple and easy to remember passwords classical password schemas no longer provide sufficient level of security for most systems.

This problem has not been ignored by researchers who are trying to create secure and easy to remember novel authentication systems or to improve existing approaches [88, 349, 343, 71, 313] . Currently most research in user authentication is geared towards graphical passwords, but such methodologies present problems of their own. In this chapter we present and compare a number of user authentication approaches, which are both easy to remember and provide very high level of security not threatened by a brute force attack with significant computational resources. After our methodologies are presented they are compared against most commonly used user authentication mechanisms in terms of how easy they are to remember and with respect to the password space size. The results of comparison are favorable for our approaches.

2. EXISTING AUTHENTICATION MECHANISMS

Many researchers have recognized inherent shortcomings of simple passwords and as a result a wealth of different authentication approaches exists. This section provides a quick overview of the most well known user authenticating techniques. We will follow a classification schema proposed by Renaud [348] in her paper on quantifying the quality of authentication mechanisms while also considering user's location as one possible, but questionable way of authenticating users.

All authentication approaches can be divided into four categories based on what a user has, knows, is or is currently located at. What the user has is typically a token or a private key and both cases while very popular are beyond the scope of this chapter.

2.1. WHERE THE USER IS LOCATED

This is an approach used mostly by online casinos to verify if the user is located in a region in which gambling operations are legal. However it does provide some level of verification of who the user is and is so included in our overview for completeness of presentation. The three approaches presented below all require additional hardware and two out of three also rely of some form of biometric for improved accuracy of user authentication. It is obvious that the geographic location alone is not sufficient information for secure user authentication, as multiple scenarios exist where an intruder may end up in approved location without being properly authorized.

2.1.1. IP filtering

This is a way to identify the location from which a user is connecting to the server, an assumption is made that if the service provider and or geographic location associated with the IP address has not changed from the last login, neither did the user identity. This is a questionable assumption and so the technology is mostly used to tell if a user is located in a locality where a certain activity such as gambling is legal, not to identify or verify users. "Where direct broadband connections such as cable modem, DSL, or T1 services are used, this mechanism is virtually foolproof. Where dialup to the ISP is used, these filtering systems lack an ability to accurately identify location. These systems can be used to allow connections through known ISP's where the final hop is hard wired. In general where this cannot be ascertained admittance is denied. As a result this is a coarse selection mechanism that will deny many users who are in fact geographically acceptable, but assures that anyone permitted within the filter is within the jurisdiction" [17].

2.1.2. GeoBio Indicator

A device consisting of an integrated Geographic Positioning System (GPS) indicator and biometric-based smart card that attaches to a personal computer via the Universal Serial Bus port. As with any standard USB plug in it is self-installing. GeoBio indicator can be used for user identification and border control, but has significant implementation costs and distribution barriers associated with hardware purchasing and distribution as well as with the enrolment process [17]. Among other problems with this approach is privacy issues inevitable raised by integration of biometric and geographic information in one data-system.

2.1.3. Phone Call Verification

Represents a method utilizing a synchronized phone call with a web session to identify user's geographic location. It even works for users with a single phone line. "During the synchronized call, [verifier] employs data matching and telephone provisioning information to determine who owns the phone and its location. A voice recording and voice biometric is captured to ensure acceptance of a transaction and limit use of an account. Country code, area code, and local exchange information can be matched to IP address providing strong location assurance. This approach offers a way to verify user's … location, in real time, without installing hardware or software on the end users computer" [17]. This approach works well for geographical location based restriction of access but it only identifies geographic location not the user, requires knowledge of English language from the user and is time consuming.

2.2. Who the user is

This is a biometrics based approach and can be extremely reliable, unfortunately physical biometrics such as fingerprints, iris scans and faces require special hardware which could be expensive to install and maintain or simply not available to all users. Behavioral biometrics based on keystroke dynamics [309], mouse usage patterns or signature dynamics do not require any special hardware and can be utilized for reliable user authentication. In this section we present two interesting user authentication schemas based on biometrics. First we introduce BioPassword a system based on keyboard dynamics followed by Pass-Thought system a proposed futuristic approach requiring special hardware to make scanning of user's thought patterns possible.

2.2.1. BioPassword

BioPassword is a patented software-only authentication system based on the keystroke dynamics biometric. While the user enters his password the system captures information about just how the user types, including any pauses between the pressings of different keys. Essentially the software observes the typing rhythm, pace and syncopation. This information is used to create a statistically reliable profile for an individual. In combination with the user's password BioPassword creates a so-called hardened password [3]. It is no longer enough to know the password itself, it is also important to enter it in precisely the same way as the true account owner would. This approach however requires an extended enrollment period.

2.2.2. Pass-Thoughts

Authors of this largely exploratory paper propose using Brain Computer Interface (BCI) technology to have a user directly transmit his thoughts to a computer [397]. The system would extract entropy from a user's brain signal upon reading a thought. The brain signals would be recorded and processed in an accurate and repeatable way providing a changeable, authentication method resilient to shoulder-surfing. The potential size of the space of a pass-thought system is not clear at this point but likely to be very large, due to the lack of bounds on what composes a thought. At the time of the publication no working model of this system exists and the whole feasibility of the approach needs to be proven.

2.3. WHAT THE USER KNOWS

This is the most popular approach and the one we are most interested in for the purpose of comparison of our approach to the existing solutions. The authentication schemas based on what a user knows can be grouped into two classes: Text based and Graphics based.

2.3.1. Text Based Approaches

Text based approaches can be further subdivided into syntactic, semantic and one-time methods. The classical passwords and passphrases are examples of syntactic methods in which a user is expected to memorize a sequence of characters or words. The sequence can either be generated for the user or user selected [348]. The problem is that user's ability to memorize complicated or multiple passwords is limited and so authentication may present problems for the user. Alternatively, easy to remember passwords are also easy to guess and so provide low level of security. Some researchers present methods, which might be easier for users to remember for example in [64] a system is presented called the Check-Off Password System (COPS) which allows users to enter characters in any order and therefore the users can choose to remember their password in many different ways. Each user is assigned 8 different characters selected from the sixteen most commonly used letters. The user may use any character more than once to form words which are easy to remember and so it is claimed COPS provides an advantage over regular passwords.

Semantic or cognitive passwords typically work by asking a user some question and treating the user's answer as the key to the authentication mechanism. One approach relies on asking the user clarifying questions until the answer matches the one expected by the system [348]. An alternative technique provided a set of questionnaires, which asked users to answer some fact-based or opinion-based questions. Those approaches are not very user friendly as it might take a long time for the user to arrive at the desired answer, and since users are very sensitive to the time component of authentication protocol, the cognitive based methods are not expected to become widely popular.

One-time password approaches are designed to provide higher level of security for crucial systems such as bank accounts. If a hacker somehow obtains a valid password he would not be able to reuse it after the initial break in. Two main approaches exist either using hardware or using codebooks, both are expensive to implement and demanding of user's time [300, 354]. In passbooks methodology a user is provided with a listing of codes, each code can be used for only a single log in. After a code is used it is crossed off and the next code becomes a valid password for the next session. After all the codes in the passbook are used a new passbook needs to be ordered. This approach clearly only works in cases where access to the system is not needed on daily bases.

2.3.2. Graphics Based Approaches

Graphical passwords are designed to take advantage of human visual memory capabilities, which are far superior to human ability to remember textual information. Two main types of graphical passwords are currently used: Recognition based and position based methods¹ are the main approaches in the current research. In the recognition based systems users have to identify images they have previously seen among new unseen before graphics.

Probably the most well known recognition based graphical authentication system is called Passfaces [20, 89]. It relies on ease with which people recognize familiar faces. During enrollment a user is presented with a set of faces he is asked to memorize. During authentication a screen with nine faces is presented to the user, with one of the faces being from his Passface set. User has to select a face, which looks familiar from the enrollment step. This process is repeated five times resulting in a relatively small space of 59050 possible face combinations. Obviously this is not sufficient if the system is open to an exhaustive search.

Another authentication system called Déjà Vu is based on Random Art images. User is asked to choose 5 images as his pass set and during authentication needs to select his pass set from a challenge set of 25 pictures. Since the pictures used are completely random and are generated by a computer program it is next to impossible to share a Déjà Vu password with others. Preliminary research shows that users prefer real photographs to random art images and that enrollment phase is more time consuming as compared to alphanumeric passwords [143].

The two systems mentioned above are probably representative of many other similar recognition based graphical authentication systems currently in existents. Visual Identification Protocol [348, 43], Picture Password [216], and PicturePins [16] all rely on exploiting user's good visual memory and power of recall to easily authenticate users by making them pick familiar images from a large set of graphics.

The remaining authentication approaches presented in this chapter are graphical position-based systems. A typical position based approach is presented in PassPoints a system based on having the user select points of interest within a single image. The number of points is not limited and so a relatively large search space is protecting against any attempt to guess a PassPoints authentication sequence [432, 434]. This is similar to the methodology used in the original patent for graphical passwords obtained by Blonder in 1996 [81].

An alternative to having a user select a portion of an image is to have a user input a simple drawing into a predefined grid space. This approach is attempted in [414] with a system called Passdoodles and also in [218, 399] with a system called Draw-a-Secret. Finally a V-go Password requests a user to perform simulation of simple actions such as mixing a cocktail using a graphical interface [348].

The aim of this overview of user authentication systems was not to produce a comprehensive listing but rather to introduce the reader to the current state of the art in the field. Many variations on the presented approaches were not described in sufficient detail and some such as textual passwords with graphical assistance [218], Authentigraph [335], Pseudoword recognition [426], Image with Sound [277], Triangle and Movable Frame schema [381], Inkblot reminder [352], Handwriting reminders [339], and Artificial Grammar Learning [426] are only mentioned here so an interested user can investigate them further.

3. SHORTCOMINGS OF THE EXISTING APPROACHES

The reason why so many different user authentication approaches exists is because all current methodologies have certain shortcomings making their use difficult or impossible for some groups of users or on some systems.

Alphanumeric passwords suffer from users picking names, simple words or their phone numbers as passwords instead of random strings making the actual password search space much smaller and so susceptible to a dictionary brute force attack. A lot of research went into limiting user's choices during enrollment process in order to make passwords more secure[73, 241, 156, 384]. For example the following set of restrictions on alphanumeric password choices is given by Klein[241]:

- Passwords based on the user's account name
- Passwords based on the user's initials or given name
- Passwords which exactly match a word in a dictionary
- Passwords which match a word in the dictionary with some or all letters capitalized
- Passwords which match a reversed word in the dictionary
- Passwords which match a reversed word in the dictionary with some or all letters capitalized
- Passwords which match a word in a dictionary with an arbitrary letter turned into a control character
- Passwords which match a dictionary word with the numbers '0', '1', '2', and '5' substituted for the letters 'o', 'l', 'z', and 's'
- Passwords which are simple conjugations of a dictionary word (i.e., plurals adding ''ing'' or ''ed'' to the end of the word, etc.)
- Passwords which are patterns from the keyboard (i.e., ''aaaaaa'' or ''qwerty'')
- Passwords which are shorter than a specific length (i.e., nothing shorter than six characters)
- Passwords which consist solely of numeric characters (i.e., Social Security numbers, telephone numbers, house addresses or office numbers)

- Passwords which do not contain mixed upper and lower case, or mixed letter and numbers, or mixed letters and punctuation
- Passwords which look like a state issued license plate number

Unfortunately those restrictions have mostly failed at creating secure but memorable alphanumeric passwords as it is beyond natural capability of human memory to easily reproduce random bits of alphanumeric information. As a result of this situation a solution was proposed which came to be known as graphical password. An approach, which is supposedly extremely easy to remember, yet at the same time is sufficiently secure. However to this day graphical passwords do not have a significant share of the authentication market potentially because they have introduced a number of new problems to the task of user identification.

Drawbacks of graphical passwords are numerous; we will start with the problems graphical passwords present to handicapped individuals. First people with impaired vision will have a problem with most graphical passwords particularly those employing images with many small details. Those users typically depend on a text reading software to interact with a computer and so would have no way of knowing what is depicted on the picture. People who have motor control problems will have a hard time precisely manipulating mouse or any other similar pointing device and so may experience some difficulty in using graphical passwords particularly those based on selection of small subparts of an image, such as PassPoints. People with certain other types of visual problems such as colorblindness may also experience problems with graphical passwords dependent on colorful images [434].

In general almost any possible user authentication approach will have a group of individuals to which such an approach presents a problem. For example Dyslexic users will have problems reading and therefore remembering text. Dyspraxics have problems with memorization of sequences, which is necessary in almost all authentication approaches reliant on sequential selection, or entry of data. Prosopagnosic people have difficulty with face recognition and so can't deal well with systems like PassFaces [348]. The only solution is to have user authentication schemas, which incorporate multiple approaches within a single user validation methodology.

Particular problems have been identified with the most of the more popular graphical password methodologies.

- In a Draw-a-Secret schema it has been shown that users tend to select drawings, which are easy to remember and as a result decrease the size of DAS password space. In particular users tend to create drawings, which are symmetric, contain only 1 to 3 strokes and are centered [317, 398]. Having this information makes a brute force attack against DAS possible.

- In an investigation of the PassPoints system it has been demonstrated that accurate recollection of the password is strongly reduced if a small tolerance region is used around the user's password points. But if a large region is used the password space of PassPoints is being reduced. Additionally it was established that not all images are suitable as PassPoints graphics. In particular images with few memorable points such as images with large expenses of green grass or overly complicated images should be avoided [433].
- A system such as PassFaces is also a subject to a reduced password space, which in case of PassFaces is already barely sufficient. It has been shown that users of a face recognition based authentication system tend to select certain faces more often than others if they are permitted to select their own passwords. In particular both males and females select attractive female faces predominantly over all other types of faces. People also tend to choose faces of people from their own race. So if the demographic information about the user is available it becomes possible to greatly narrow the password space for a system like PassFaces. If the system does not permit users to select their own passwords it becomes more difficult for users to remember such faces as they often are from a different race and so more difficult to distinguish and remember [135].

Another significant drawback of graphical passwords is the so-called shoulder surfing problem. While in alphanumeric authentication schemas it is easily solved with a replacement of the password with a familiar star pattern [******], the situation is much harder for graphical passwords. A person who observes a few login sessions could eventually realize what the password is or obtain information making guessing of the password much easier. Sobrado et al. propose a shoulder-surfing-secure graphical password schema but it requires over a 1000 small pictures to be displayed on a single screen making it impossible to use on most portable devices and a nightmare for people with impaired vision [381]. Additionally a lengthy, 10 step, sequence is required for secure authentication. A similar but somewhat modified approach is presented in Hoanca et al. [197] and a broad overview of solutions to the shoulder surfing problem is given by Li et al. [272].

4. PASSTEXT

We propose a novel approach to user authentication, which addresses some of the limitations of current password schemes both graphical and textual. We call our approach PassText and as the name implies it is a close relative of both passwords and PassPhrases. In fact it takes the difference between passwords and passphrases to the next level. Some work in this direction for text-based passwords has been started by [218] who proposed a scheme for combining textual passwords with predefined simple graphical input displays allowing a user to input the same password in multiple locations. Similarly in [399] researchers present an approach for selecting between different grid spaces for input of graphical passwords.

Ideally we want our passphrases to be as long as is humanly possible to remember making them impossible to guess by brute force or other means. At the same time the users should not easily forget their passphrases or parts thereof as time from the initial enrollment step passes. It is not reasonable to expect a user to remember or to have to type in any passphrase longer than a dozen of words. So what we propose, is instead of having the burden of providing the passphrase rest on the user's shoulders it should be instead stored and readily available in the user authentication system itself.

At the PassText creation stage also known as the enrolment stage the user is presented with a large body of text to which he is asked to make any modifications he pleases. A possible list of atomic modification includes:

- Deleting any character from the text
- Typing any character in any location

Obviously a combination of the above modifications with possible repetitions can be used to produce a unique PassText. A user can delete whole paragraphs, move around sections of the text, replace words with different ones, and replace capitalization of individual characters and so on. Basically any standard word processing operation can be utilized. A resulting PassText is just a very long string of characters, which for simplicity is restricted to being plain text. The PassText acts just like any simple text string, deleting a character causes all following characters to shift one character to the left and the size of the PassText decreases by one. The opposite is also true, adding a character shifts all the following character to the right and increases the size of PassText by one. To insure that the user has correctly entered his desired PassText we might ask him to repeat it again during the enrollment stage and set it up only if the verification is successfully performed.

A potential search space for classical passwords is considered to be secure as long as the users select passwords with equal probability from all possible combinations of characters. However in reality many short, simple passwords are used making it possible to guess them or to find them by a brute force attack. Perhaps a similar problem may take place with the PassText system. Users may attempt to save time by making only minimum changes to the base text or not making any changes at all. The system should require a minimum number of atomic operations before a new PassText is approved. PassTexts created by making no changes to the text, deleting just one word in the text or one block of text or just a single character should not be allowed.

In the PassText system of authentication the user is not required to memorize any difficult character combinations such as "D@$0o#bk2", in fact the user is not required to memorize any text at all, he is however free to do so. User only needs to memorize the sequence of changes he makes to the base document. We argue that this is relatively easy since working with documents is something many computer users frequently do anyways. Also the choice of the base document can be made to reflect user's previous knowledge without sacrificing the security aspect of the system. In fact a system can be designed with customizable options for each user:

1. The default option is for all users to be presented with a common text. For example the Declaration of Independence can serve as a widely known base text document.

2. A user can select an option of having his user name associated with a particular text from a list of possible base text (a more secure but less convenient option is for user to select a text from a larger list of texts).

3. Another option is for a user to provide his own base text file, but this might be a problem for login from remote systems, which may not have immediate access to the user's chosen base text file due to limited resources particularly in the case of small mobile devices.

An observant reader has probably noticed that it is possible to use multiple-base-text-selection-menu to create PassTexts made up of the parts of multiple documents with a simple copy and paste command sequence. However this is not necessary as the PassText security is inherently very strong. In a relatively short text of just one page we have up to 80 characters per line and about 40 lines per page, for example this page of text you are currently reading contains around 2500 characters. Assuming a very small alphabet of only 64 characters we have a total possible PassText space of 64^{2500},which is enough to disillusion any potential hacker.

However, PassText system does not explicitly limit the size of the base texts, which can be used. Depending on the desired level of security any written work can be utilized as a base text from paper abstract to a whole set of encyclopedias. Then again, it is unlikely for any application to require such extremely high level of security or for any user to select a modification that deep within the base text. In fact it is probably unreasonable to expect a user to scroll through more than a few pages within the base text and so the practical PassText space is not likely to ever be much over 64^{5000} as the text beyond the first two pages is likely to remain unchanged and simply shifted forward. Obviously this cannot be considered a limitation of PassText system, as the security is still many orders of magnitude beyond all other currently used authentication schemes. Theoretically however we can take an alphabet of 96 characters and use a small book of perhaps a million characters long to give as a PassText space which would not be fully searchable in any realistic amount of time.

Perhaps an example is in order to demonstrate how the system works and what kind of PassTexts users can generate. Continuing with our example of Declaration of Independence as the base text and shortening it for illustration purposes we have the text on the left side of the following figure. On the right hand side is the PassText created by removing the word "dissolve" from the first sentence of the base text and replacing it with a last word of the base text namely word "world". Both sides of the figure look fairly similar to the user since they are presented as a formatted text, but to the system, which sees them as strings, they are drastically different both in size and in makeup.

While the number of possible base text manipulation is truly enormous we would like to reiterate that memorizing the actual sequence leading to the creation of a secure PassText is very easy and can even be done for authentication on multiple systems with multiple base texts without any additional memorization being required. For example your PassText might be to replace first occurrence of the letter "a" in a base text with a word "USA" which is very easy to remember.

Additionally the PassText technology is not very susceptible to "shoulder surfing" as can be clearly seen from Figure 1. Noticing a single new word in a large body of text or even an absence of some word in a text is not a trivial task particularly if the PassText is created by modifying multiple pages in the base text not all visible on the screen at the same time. While it is common to use asterisks [******] to prevent others from viewing your password it is not a very good idea in the case of PassText as the formation easily draws attention and can help a hacker identify a region which needs to be explored using brute force for a potential guess of your PassText.

PassText is also better than graphical passwords since storing and manipulating text requires fewer resources than working with images. In fact it takes only a few kilobytes of space to store a PassText base text of two pages, but a complicated high-resolution graphical password may require multiple megabytes of storage. This is particularly important in the case of small screen devices, such as cell phones, on which resolution is not sufficient to display high content graphics. Unlike graphics, text is also readable by the special software used by the blind people to interact with a computer, making it usable for people with impaired vision. PassText requires no color comprehension and so is friendly towards the color blind. Finally it is much easier to manipulate text as compared to graphics making it better for people with poor motor coordination. Overall PassText is a much more handicapped friendly technology as compared to typical graphical password approaches.

When in the Course of human events, it becomes necessary for one people to dissolve the political bands which have connected them with another, and to assume among the powers of the earth, the separate and equal station to which the Laws of Nature and of Nature's God entitle them, a decent respect to the opinions of mankind requires that they should declare the causes which impel them to the separation. We hold these truths to be self-evident, that all men are created equal, that they are endowed by their Creator with certain unalienable Rights, that among these are Life, Liberty and the pursuit of Happiness. --That to secure these rights, Governments are instituted among Men, deriving their just powers from the consent of the governed, -- That whenever any Form of Government becomes destructive of these ends, it is the Right of the People to alter or to abolish it, and to institute new Government, laying its foundation on such principles and organizing its powers in such form, as to them shall seem most likely to effect their Safety and Happiness. Prudence, indeed, will dictate that Governments long established should not be changed for light and transient causes; and accordingly all experience hath shewn, that mankind are more disposed to suffer, while evils are sufferable, than to right themselves by abolishing the forms to which they are accustomed. But when a long train of abuses and usurpations, pursuing invariably the same Object evinces a design to reduce them under absolute Despotism, it is their right, it is their duty, to throw off such Government, and to provide new Guards for their future security.	When in the Course of human events, it becomes necessary for one people to world the political bands which have connected them with another, and to assume among the powers of the earth, the separate and equal station to which the Laws of Nature and of Nature's God entitle them, a decent respect to the opinions of mankind requires that they should declare the causes which impel them to the separation. We hold these truths to be self-evident, that all men are created equal, that they are endowed by their Creator with certain unalienable Rights, that among these are Life, Liberty and the pursuit of Happiness. --That to secure these rights, Governments are instituted among Men, deriving their just powers from the consent of the governed, -- That whenever any Form of Government becomes destructive of these ends, it is the Right of the People to alter or to abolish it, and to institute new Government, laying its foundation on such principles and organizing its powers in such form, as to them shall seem most likely to effect their Safety and Happiness. Prudence, indeed, will dictate that Governments long established should not be changed for light and transient causes; and accordingly all experience hath shewn, that mankind are more disposed to suffer, while evils are sufferable, than to right themselves by abolishing the forms to which they are accustomed. But when a long train of abuses and usurpations, pursuing invariably the same Object evinces a design to reduce them under absolute Despotism, it is their right, it is their duty, to throw off such Government, and to provide new Guards for their future security.

Figure 5.1: Left: Declaration of Independence; Right: PassText example

It is possible to develop a much more complicated and as a result more secure PassText model based on full capabilities of an advanced word processor such as setting different styles of the document, using different fonts, various sizes of characters and even different colors of individual letters. Most readers of this chapter should be fairly familiar with modern word processors and understand how many text-formatting possibilities they present. However those additional features are purely optional as the PassText system is designed to work perfectly well within the limitations of simple plain-text manipulating software.

5. PASSART

Another novel user authentication approach can be based on what is commonly known as "ASCII art" [1]. ASCII art is a graphic made out of individual characters placed together and selected from the standard 95 character printable alphabet defined by American Standard Code for Information Interchange (ASCII). Two approaches to creation of ASCII images are known: either an artist manually places characters in a desired location or a computer program converts a given image file by sampling it and replacing individual pixels or pixel-regions with ASCII characters. Figure 5.2 shows an ASCII representation of an image file created by one of many ASCII art generating programs [1, 436].

Figure 5.2: Original Image; Right: ASCII representation

The actual algorithm for generating ASCII art is beyond the scope of this chapter, but it is sufficient to say what many algorithms exist and public domain converters are widely available [1]. Any image can be used as the base image regardless of color, complexity or size for creation of ASCII art for esthetic purposes, however for our purpose of user authentication we would like to have a base image, which is not very high in resolution or picture size. This is needed to have the resulting ASCII text easily fit into a single screen with individual characters easily visible.

From that point on PassArt works a lot like PassText. At the PassArt creation stage also known as the enrolment stage the user is presented with a sample of ASCII art to which he is asked to make any modifications he pleases.

In the PassArt system of authentication the user is not required to memorize any difficult character combinations, in fact the user is not required to memorize any text at all. User only needs to memorize the locations within the base art piece he makes the changes to. We argue that this is relatively easy since it relies on user's visual memory, which is known to be very long lasting and partially subconscious.

PassArt system does not explicitly limit the size of the base art, which can be used, depending on the desired level of security any image can be utilized as a base art from a small drawing to a Michelangelo's ceiling in the Sistine Chapel. Overall PassArt provides a passwords space, which can't be searched with current computational resources. We can take an alphabet of all 95 printable characters and use a large painting made up of perhaps a million different characters giving as a PassArt space, which would not be fully searchable till the end of time.

Figure 5.3 gives an example of how the system works and what kind of PassArt users can utilize. Due to the limited size of PassArt we can incorporate into this publication, the example is trivial and manually produced [10]. For real life use much larger and automatically generated ASCII art pieces should be used, consisting of multiple characters. Given a picture of a house and a tree as a base art piece a user can for example create a simple PassArt by changing part of the roof to a text "BUFFALOCS", which should be relatively easy to remember for someone attending Buffalo university. Any other simple word would do, or nothing at all as it is sufficient to simply delete different aspects of the base art. One may find it easier to simply remove the front window from the house all together as his unique and easy to remember PassArt.

```
  XXXXXXXXXXXXXX          XXXXX              XXXXXXXXXXXXXX          XXXXX
  XXXXXXXXXXXXXXXX       XXXXXXXXX           XXXXXXXXXXXXXXXX       XXXXXXXXX
  XXXXXXXXXXXXXX   XX    XXXXXXXXXXX         XXXXBUFFALOCS    XX    XXXXXXXXXXX
  XXXXXXXXXXXXXX      XX XXXXXXXXXXX         XXXXXXXXXXXXXX      XX XXXXXXXXXXX
  XXXXXXXXXXXXXX      XX XXXXXXXXX           XXXXXXXXXXXXXX      XX XXXXXXXXX
  X            X      X  XXXXX               X            X      X  XXXXX
  X  XX  XX  X  XXX   X     X                X  XX  XX  X  XXX   X     X
  X  XX  XX  X  XXX   X     X                X  XX  XX  X  XXX   X     X
  X         X  XXX    X     X                X         X  XXX    X     X
  XXXXXXXXXXXXXXXXXXXXXXX         X          XXXXXXXXXXXXXXXXXXXXXXX         X
```

Figure 5.3: Left: base ASCII image; Right: PassArt example

6. PASSMAP

One of the main problems with passwords is that very good passwords are hard to remember and the ones which are easy to remember are too short of simple to be secure. From the studies of human memory we know that it is relatively easy to remember landmarks on a well-known journey [13]. Perhaps we can design an authentication schema based around this idea, a password which would be easy to remember and relatively quick to provide to the system, while at the same time is impossible to break with brute force alone.

The Traveling Salesman Problem or TSP as it is known, is a classical NP-Hard problem in which a salesperson is trying to find the shortest path for visiting N cities. The formal definition of the problem states: "Find a path through a weighted graph which starts and ends at the same vertex, includes every other vertex exactly once, and minimizes the total cost of edges"[78]. Numerous approaches for solving the TSP exist, but only the brute force approach provides optimal solutions, but as a result of the magnitude of the search space it is not an option to use the brute force approach for any reasonably large network of cities.

For user authentication we are not really concerned with solving TSP or even with the efficiency of any particular route. We are only interested in utilization of the large search space inherent in the TSP problem and the ease of memorization of routes enjoyed by the human long-term memory system. Initially for our user authentication system we considered having a user provide a path among N cities as his unique access code we call a PassMap. This approach is not very user friendly, as it requires the user to remember and input a long sequence of routes between cities. An alternative would be to have some path between N cities already provided to the user and have the user make changes to the route to personalize it. This also creates a problem, as a large number of changes are needed to make the resulting path not easily discovered by brute force approach given that the original provided tour is known.

The solution we found is to relax the requirement for PassMap to visit all N cities [445]. A user is shown a map of some N cities with some routes selected and all other routes between all cities available but not activated. If we treat N given cities as edges in a complete graph it has N(N-1)/2 undirected edges. In a relatively standard map of just 50 cities, we have about $2^{50(50-1)/2} = 2^{1225}$ possible edge combinations. The user's PassMap consists of some modifications to the given map of routes, or in more precise terms of the set of selected and not selected edges in a sub-graph of the whole map. Since the search space is really enormous it is safe for the user to make relatively few modifications to the base map and as a result have no problems with their memorization. Additionally PassMap system does not explicitly limit the size of the base map, which can be used; depending on the desired level of security any map can be utilized as a base map from a small town to a map of a whole continent with hundreds of cities. Then again, it is unlikely for any application to require such extremely high level of security.

At the PassMap creation stage also known as the enrolment stage the user is presented with a relatively large map of routes to which he is asked to make any modifications he pleases A possible list of atomic modifications includes:

- Selecting a direct route between any two cities
- Un-selecting a direct route between any two cities

Obviously a combination of the above modifications with possible repetitions can be used to produce a unique PassMap. A user can delete whole routes, make certain cities inaccessible, provide multiple paths between any two cities and so on. A resulting PassMap is just a set of edges of a graph. To insure that the user has correctly entered his desired PassMap we might ask him to repeat it again during the enrollment stage and set it up only if the verification is successfully performed. The map itself is trivial to generate by using a simple random number generator, which assigns each possible edge to either activated or deactivated mode. Once generated such map can be reused for multiple users and in multiple systems without any additional processing being required.

Figure 5.4 demonstrate how the system works and what kind of PassMaps users can generate. Due to the limited size of maps we can incorporate into this publication, the example is simple and manually produced [7]. Suppose the user is presented with a map of all 50 US states with their capitals and some routes indicated as shown in Figure 5.4 (top). The user has great memories of Santa Fe, Austin, Honolulu and Phoenix, perhaps he met his wife in Sante Fe, his parents are from Austin, he went to school in Phoenix and always dreamed of going to Hawaii. He decided to create his PassMap by making a complete graph of those four cities or in plain terms connecting them in every way possible. Since Phoenix and Honolulu and Honolulu and Phoenix are already connected he only needs to add the four remaining edges to create his own unique PassMap. Ideally of course users should not utilize their personal information in generation of their password since someone who knows them well might be able to guess it. As an alternative example we can use a map of Europe and a user who has never been to Europe before should have no problem memorizing that he wants to one day see the Eiffel Tour in Paris, the Big Ben in London and the Kremlin in Moscow and his PassMap might be to visit all of them one at a time flying in from his hometown.

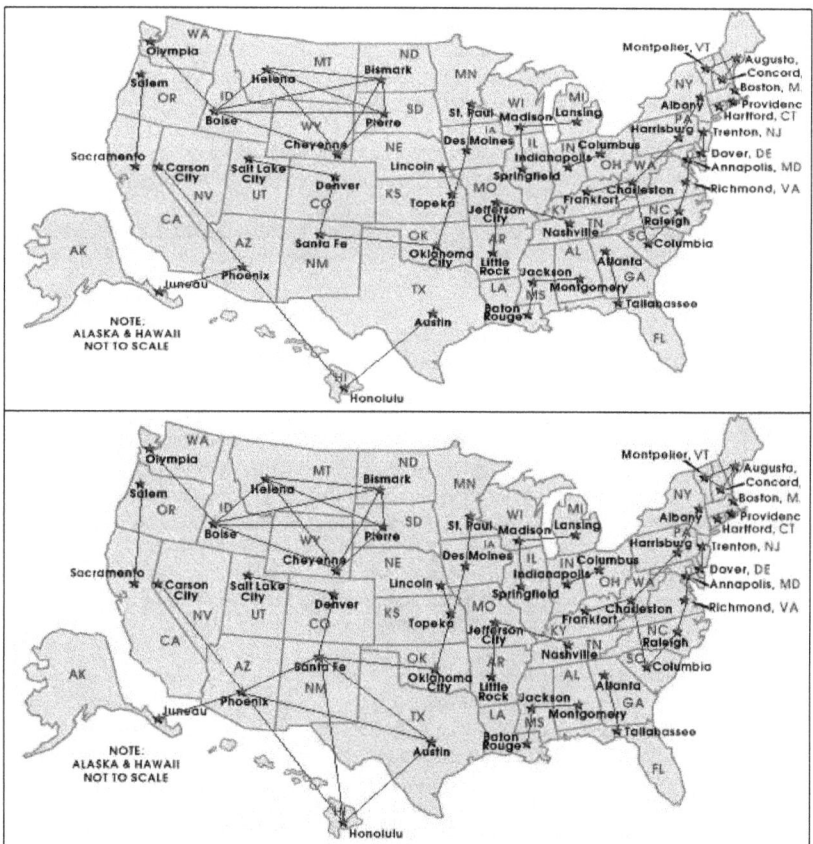

Figure 5.4: Top: Given base map; Bottom: PassMap example [7]

While the number of possible base map manipulations is truly enormous we would like to reiterate that memorizing the actual sequence leading to the creation of a secure PassMap is very easy and can even be done for authentication on multiple systems with multiple base maps without any additional memorization being required. For example your PassMap might be to connect the most upper-left city with the lowest city and with most upper-right city regardless of the actual map presented to you. Additionally the PassMap technology is not very susceptible to "shoulder surfing" as can be clearly seen from Figure 4. Noticing a single new edge in a large graph or even an absence of some edge in the map is not a trivial task.

7. RESULTS AND CONCLUSIONS

It seems unfair to say that any n alphanumeric characters are equally easy to commit to memory. For example "Ffi0o" and word "black" are not both equal to five units of memory. We propose a new measure of password length based on a unit of memorable information (UMI). A single word is just a single UMI since we do not memorize the characters in the word one at a time, but rather as a whole. In a similar fashion a single picture or a single point in a picture is also one UMI, just like recognition of a single face is. With respect to our PassText, PassArt and PassMap algorithms a single change to the base information is also a single unit of memorable information and should be treated as such for comparison purposes with other authentication techniques.

By comparing password space for different password schemas we can identify the most secure approaches with respect to brute force attacks while at the same time considering how good those mechanisms are in terms of how memorable they are.

Table 5.1 demonstrates comparison of password space and password length for popular user authentication schemas and for the approaches proposed in this chapter.

Table 5.1 shows that approaches presented by us are both the most secure and easiest to remember, while at the same time are relatively fast to produce during authentication procedure. PassText and PassArt do not require unreasonable graphical or computational resources and PassMap is inherently easy to remember. Each one of the proposed methods may be easier for people with certain disabilities to utilize as compared to some other authentication approaches.

Authentication System	Alphabet	Password Length in UMI	Password Space Size
Password[0]	64	8 (chars)	2.8×10^{14}
Password	72	8 (chars)	7.2×10^{14}
Password	96	8 (chars)	7.2×10^{15}
PassPhrase[1]	50000	5 (words)	3.1×10^{23}
PassPoints[2]	373	5 (clicks)	7.2×10^{12}
PassPoints[3]	1925	5 (clicks)	2.6×10^{16}
PassPoints[4]	3928	5 (clicks)	9.3×10^{17}
Pin Number[5]	10	4 (numbers)	1×10^{4}
Text with Graphical Assistance[6]	10 (spaces)	8 (chars)	2×10^{6}
DAS[6]	5 x 5 grid	5 (elements)	5×10^{5}
DAS	5 x 5 grid	6 (elements)	1.7×10^{7}
DAS	5 x 5 grid	7 (elements)	6×10^{8}
Picture Password[7]	30	8 (selections)	6.5×10^{11}
Daja Vu	20	5 (images)	1.5×10^{4}
PassFace	9	5 (faces)	5.9×10^{4}
Check-Off Password	16	4 (check-offs)	1.2×10^{4}
Check-Off Password[8]	16	4 (check-offs)	7.2×10^{16}
PassThought[9]	95	8 (chars)	6.6×10^{15}
PassText[10]	95	2 (changes)	2.6×10^{494}
PassText[11]	95	3 (changes)	95^{1250}
PassText[12]	95	4 (changes)	95^{2500}
PassArt[13]	95	2 (changes)	2.6×10^{494}
PassArt[14]	95	3 (changes)	95^{1250}
PassArt[15]	95	4 (changes)	95^{2500}
PassMap[16]	10	2 (changes)	3.5×10^{13}
PassMap	25	3 (changes)	2×10^{90}
PassMap	50	3 (changes)	2^{1225}

0: see [434] for details. 1: 50000 dictionary words are taken as a working vocabulary of an adult. 2: image size 451 x 331 with grid size of 20 x 20 pixels [434]. 3: image size 1024 x 752 with grid size of 20 x 20 pixels [434]. 4: image size 1024 x 752 with grid size of 14 x 14 pixels [434]. 5: see [43] for details. 6: see [218] for details. 7: see [216] for details. 8: if OCR not possible see [64] for details. 9: proposed system currently not feasible [397]. 10: 250 chars. 11: half page of text (1250 chars). 12: 1 page of text (2500 chars). 13: 250 char ASCII art piece. 14: half page ASCII art (1250 chars). 15: 1 page ASCII art (2500 chars). 16: for N cities we have $2^{N(N-1)/2}$ password space.

Table 5.1: Comparison of password space and password length for popular user authentication schemas and for the approaches proposed in this chapter

PassArt is a particularly handicapped-friendly methodology since it combines positive properties of both graphical and alphanumeric passwords. By doing so it provides a choice to the user of either relying on image or textual manipulation for entry of the password sequence depending on the nature of their disability. In terms of the password space all three approaches exhibit a password space, which is sufficient to make a brute force attack impossible. With respect to memorization, all our methods require fewer UMI than currently utilized approaches making it easier for the user to keep track of his authentication code. Field trials are required to determine which of the three-presented approaches are preferable for use with small mobile devices.

With the goal of total computer and network security user authentication is only the first step. A good intruder detection mechanism is also required to protect the system against those who were able to defeat its identification mechanisms. Our research outlined in presents a system for continuous user verification based on user's behavior and promises to provide improved system security then coupled with one of the proposed user authentication approaches.

CHAPTER 6 - ANALYZING USER PASSWORD SELECTION BEHAVIOR FOR REDUCTION OF PASSWORD SPACE

"To predict the behavior of ordinary people in advance, you only have to assume that they will always try to escape a disagreeable situation with the smallest possible expenditure of intelligence"

Friedrich Nietzsche (1844 – 1900)

Abstract—*This chapter presents a comprehensive survey of recent literature on the topic of password dictionaries for alphanumeric and graphical user authentication approaches including some password schemas proposed by the author. After different methods used for reduction of password space are introduced, they are analyzed and compared with the intent of finding a common flaw of user authentication mechanisms, which allows for the development of such password dictionaries by hackers. Our conclusion is that any user authentication system, which allows users to exercise choice in selection of their passwords, is vulnerable to the password space reduction methods presented in this chapter and so should not be utilized.*

1. INTRODUCTION

In the past few years a lot of research went into analyzing and classifying user's choices of passwords [241, 156, 73, 313, 92]. Such research has benefits ranging from better understanding of personality types [92], to increasing security and reliability of computer systems and networks. Passwords are based on secret, often-personal information, which is frequently intrinsically linked to the person generating it. Clever hackers are learning to utilize such a connection to improve their chances of breaking into computer systems as well as increasing computational resources available to them [321, 334]. In order to combat such personalized attacks we need to better understand what types of password dictionaries currently exist, and which can appear in the near future. Such knowledge can allow us to improve our security procedures and perhaps develop superior novel user authentication mechanism resistant to dictionary based attacks [72].

2. PASSWORD SPACE REDUCTION TECHNIQUES

The following sections describe different tendencies of user's in various authentication mechanisms, which can be utilized to reduce the overall password space, making the mentioned password systems unreliable for system protection and accessibly to the brute force attacks.

2.1 ALPHANUMERIC PASSWORDS

It has been shown that passwords can be grouped into four broad categories: family oriented, fans, fantasies, and cryptic [92]. "Family oriented" users, which comprise 47.5% of users, select their own name or last name or other personal information such as pet or child's name as their password. Those are usually less experienced computer users. "Fans" utilize celebrities as passwords and comprise another 32% of users. Those are often younger computer users. "Fantasy" group relies on expressing their imagination and desire by selecting passwords such as "hot" and is comprised of about 11% of users. Remaining 9.5% of users are sophisticated computer users who understand security and tend to select truly difficult to guess random passwords. It is the first three groups, which are a target of concentrated dictionary attacks. The rest of this section goes into particular details of passwords, which can be found in those categories.

A lot of research has gone into identifying commonly used alphanumeric passwords [82, 76, 385, 379, 236]. Large dictionaries composing many possible passwords are freely available on the Internet. Those dictionaries taken together with personal information about the user are often sufficient to relatively quickly break between 20 and 30 percent of all passwords used in a given system by simple trial and error approach. By analyzing different types of passwords found in different systems the following suggestions can be made to attempt to reduce the passwords search space for alphanumeric-textual authentication approaches [241]:

- First try all the available personal information about the user such as: "one's names and initials; One's account name; Names of immediate family members;

Names, breeds or species of pets; One's birthday; Family member's birthdays; One's vehicle make, model, year; Hobbies, interests and related words; One's job title; Employer's name; Job related words; Friend's names; Street numbers or names, city, county, state or zip code for home, work, family or friends; Phone numbers for home, work, family or friends; Social security numbers for self and immediate family; License plate numbers; Birthplace including street address; University or college name; College major; High school name; Student or employee ID numbers; Serial numbers from consumer products"

- Words from a number of dictionaries including technical and professional dictionaries
- List of personal names
- Listing of geographical terms such as countries, cities, lakes, rivers, etc.
- List of celebrity names, movie stars, writers, scientists, philosophers, athletes, sports team names
- Listing of characters from books, movies, cartoons, plays, mythology, religious texts
- Different numbers both spelled out and as numerals, repetitive strings of characters, common keyboard patterns,
- Short common phrases, word pairs and triples
- Common abbreviations and mnemonics
- For foreign users try a dictionary of foreign words in English transliteration.

Length	Percentage [384]	Percentage [241]
1	0.4%	0.1%
2	0.6%	0.2%
3	1.53%	2.0%
4	3.25%	5.7%
5	9.86%	9.5%
6	22.01%	34.7%
7	21.15%	24.4%
8	41.86%	23.4%

Table 6.1: Average length of passwords (based on [241] and [384])

For each type of password guesses given above a number of variations should also be tried such as: "append or prepend defined characters to a word; Reverse a word; Duplicate a word; Append the reversed word; Rotate a word either left or right, i.e. move the first letter to the end or the last letter to the front; Upper case a word; Lower case a word; Make only the first letter a capital; Make all but the first letter a capital; Toggle the case of all characters; Toggle the case of a character at a set position; Minimum and maximum word lengths can be set or long words can be truncated at a set length; Suffixes may be added to words; First, last or any specific character may be deleted; Characters can be replaced at a set location; Characters can be inserted at a set location; "Shift" the case, i.e. substitute the other character on the same key, e.g. 'a' and 'A' or '5' and '%'; Shift the characters left or right by keyboard position (so an 's' becomes an 'a' or 'd'); Replace all of one character with another; Replace all characters of a class (for example vowels, letters, non letters, digits) with a specific character; Remove all occurrences of any character from a word; Remove all characters of a class from a word. [369]"

Additional analysis of known passwords can allow for classification by frequency of passwords with regard to types described above. In terms of the character length Table 6.1 demonstrates password distribution which has been experimentally observed by [384] and [241] respectively. With respect to the password makeup in terms of constituting characters the following statistics have been calculated:

Characters	Percentage
Lower-case only	28.9%
Mixed Case	38.1%
Some upper-case	40.9%
Digits	31.7%
Meta-characters	0.2%
Control characters	1.4%
Space and/or tab	4.1%
. , ;	6.1%
- _ = +	1.6%
!#$%^&*()	4.7%
Other non-alphanumeric characters	1.7%

Table 6.2: Password makeup (taken from [384])

In case of passwords based on the words in a foreign language the following distribution was observed [384].

Language	Percentage
Australian/Aboriginal	.96%
Danish	2.8%
Dutch	2.2%
English	13%
Finnish	7.7%
French	2.6%
German	2.8%
Italian	7.9%
Japanese	4.5%
Norwegian	2.6%
Swedish	1.9%

Table 6.3: Passwords by language (taken from [384])

Some languages were not considered which in environments rich with foreign speakers might be particularly beneficial such as trying Asian (Chinese, Korean), Indian and Russian languages in systems frequently used by computer scientists. Other types of easily cracked passwords can be summarized as follows [241]:

Type of Password	Percentage
User/account name	2.7%
Character sequence	.2%
Numbers	.1%
Chinese	.4%
Place names	.6%
Common names	4.0%
Female names	1.2%
Male names	1%
Uncommon names	.9%
Myths & legends	.5%
Shakespearean	.1%
Sports teams	.2%
Science fiction	.4%
Movie and actors	.1%
Cartoons	.1%
Famous people	.4%
Phrases and patterns	1.8%
Surnames	.1%
Biology	.007%
/usr/dict/words	7.4%
Machine names	1%
Mnemonics	.014%
King James bible	.6%
Miscellaneous words	.4%
Asteroids	.1%

Table 6.4: Passwords by type of information (taken from [241])

2.2 PASSFACES

A system such as Passfaces [20] has an inherently small password space which creators claim is sufficient since no known dictionary exists for such type of password making further reduction of password space impossible. However, recent research [309] suggests otherwise.

While no pre-computed dictionary currently exists for Passfaces user preferences can be used to greatly reduce the size of search space in face recognition based authentication systems. It has been demonstrated that faces selected are affected by the race of the user and a strong preference is shown for attractive faces. Also, all users show preference for female faces. In case of male users preference for selecting attractive female faces is so strong that it makes password space manually searchable for Passface-like systems [309].

By knowing some demographic information about the user hacker can greatly reduce password space he has to search. If a user is male the search space for the worst 10% of passwords is equal to two. In case of Asian users of known gender search space is just one for the easiest 10% of passwords! Figures below demonstrate just how extreme user's facial biases can be [309].

User	Female Model	Male Model	Typical Female	Typical Male
Female	40.0%	20.0%	28.8%	11.3%
Male	63.2%	10.0%	12.7%	14.0%

Table 6.5: Facial preferences by gender (taken from [309])

Users of both genders tend to select female faces much more frequently (68% for females and 75% for males). Males also almost 5 times more likely to select attractive females as apposed to average looking ones.

User	Asian	Black	White
Asian female	52.1%	16.7%	31.3%
Asian male	34.4%	21.9%	43.8%
Black male	8.3%	91.7%	0.0%
White female	18.8%	31.3%	50.0%
White male	17.6%	20.4%	62.0%

Table 6.6: Facial preferences by race (taken from [309])

As far as race was concerned users tended to selected faces corresponding to their own race. Asian females and White females did so 50% of the time, White males 60% of the time and Black males 90% of the time.

2.3 STORY

In the story authentication approach a user has to select a sequence of themed images [135]. The differences between males and females are not extreme, but still statistically significant. Females tend to choose animals twice as often as males do, while males show preference for choosing pictures of women twice as much. Other less significant differences are presented in the Figures below and show how the two genders and three different races differ in terms of preferences for different themes.

User	Female	Male
Animals	20.8%	10.4%
Cars	14.6%	17.9%
Women	6.3%	13.6%
Food	14.6%	11.0%
Children	8.3%	6.8%
Men	4.2%	4.6%
Objects	12.5%	11.0%
Nature	14.6%	17.2%
Sports	4.2%	7.5%

Table 6.7: Topic preferences by gender (taken from [135])

User	Asian	Hispanic	White
Animals	10.7%	12.5%	12.5%
Cars	18.6%	12.5%	16.8%
Women	11.4%	25.0%	13.0%
Food	11.4%	12.5%	11.5%
Children	8.6%	0.0%	6.3%
Men	4.3%	12.5%	11.5%
Nature	17.1%	12.5%	11.1%

Table 6.8: Topic preferences by race (take from [135])

Utilizing the demographic information presented above for the easiest 10% of passwords, which belonged to Asian males, it was shown to be possible to break the Story authentication mechanism in just twenty attempts [135].

2.4 DRAW-A-SECRET

Recent investigation of types of drawings users tend to select as their draw-a-secret passwords revealed some common properties which can be taken advantage of by a clever hacker in order to reduce password space of a draw-a-secret approaches [317, 398]. Drawings can be classified into three groups based on the following characteristics: global symmetry, number of strokes and location within the grid.

Vertical Reflective	19%
Horizontal Reflective	8%
Diagonal Reflective	4%
Total Reflective	31%
Rotational	7%
Repetitive	7%
Total Symmetric	45%
Total Asymmetric	55%

Table 6.9: Symmetry for draw-a-secret passwords (taken from [317])

1-3 strokes	4-6 strokes	> 6 strokes
80%	10%	10%

Table 6.10: Number of strokes in a draw-a-secret code (taken from [317])

Centered	Approximately Centered	Not Centered
56%	30%	14%

Table 6.11: Location of a d.a.s. password on a grid (taken from [317])

As can be see from the above figures, 45% of users tend to choose symmetric passwords, with 66% of those being reflective. A large majority of users (80%) have a relatively short password of 1 to 3 strokes and another 56% of users locate their drawings in a center of a grid or almost the center for an additional 30% of users [317].

2.5 PASSPOINTS

In an investigation of the PassPoints system it has been demonstrated that accurate recollection of the password is strongly reduced if a small tolerance region is used around the user's password points. But if a large region is used the password space of PassPoints is being reduced. Additionally it was established that not all images are suitable as PassPoints graphics. In particular images with few memorable points such as images with large expenses of green grass or overly complicated images should be avoided. One reason being that large regions with little character such as blue sky can be safely eliminated as potentially containing pass points. The opposite is also true, a really memorable region such as a small boat in an ocean is very likely to be chosen by the users as the pass point. So the overall password space of PassPoints can be greatly reduced by not considering large fields with monotonous information, and concentrating on potential regions of interest to a user, such as faces, outlier objects based on color or size and other easy to remember sub-parts of an image [433].

2.6 PRONOUNCEABLE PASSWORDS

Random pronounceable passwords are automatically generated by computer programs to assist users in obtaining a secure password, which is also relatively easy to remember. It has been shown by Ganesan et al. [169] that based on a particular implementation of a random pronounceable password generator it might be possible to greatly reduce the overall password space.

While different passwords have an equal probability of being generated in each of the possible categories, because of the additional knowledge about distribution of vowels, consonants, etc. in pronounceable words it is possible to select a category with a small overall number of possible passwords, but which nonetheless has the same total number of passwords as all the other categories. As a result average density of passwords per unit of password space in such a sub-space is extremely high. Unlike in other password dictionaries hacker does not generate a list of likely passwords, but rather determines a relatively small region in a password space, which is likely to contain many user passwords. So while the overall password space of the generator may be practically un-searchable, a small sub-space may be a fruitful ground for a brute force attack [169].
As long as the objective of the hacker is not to break into a particular account but into any account in the system this approach works extremely well, to the point there continuous use of password generators of this type is not recommended by authors of the study [169].

2.7 PASSTEXT

A recently developed system proposed by the author relies on manipulation of free-form text by the user. It has been investigated with respect to common tendencies of users. Results similar to those from investigation of alphanumeric passwords have been obtained. Users typically added personal information such as name or date of birth in case they chose to add text. As far as removing parts of text, the actual text being removed depended on the text itself, but easy to remember locations were often selected, such as title of the text, and first or last sentence of the text.

2.8 PASSMAP

Another user authentication mechanism proposed by the author is based on selection of routes in a map. It has been put through a preliminary testing and while the set of test users was limited to just a dozen, it was shown that users tended to select locations, which they have visited or wanted to visit. Particularly places of birth showed a high degree of being selected. Also famous locations were chosen more often than less known ones.

3. CONCLUSIONS

Users have long been considered the weakest component of any security system [90, 427, 220, 194]. Across different authentication schemas users tend to choose passwords, which are easy to remember, and so are easy to guess. In addition users show strong preference for egocentric passwords based on their own names in case of alphanumeric passwords, faces of the same race as they are in case of face-recognition based authentication schemas and personal information in case of PassText or PassMap systems. Table 6.12 summarizes the types of information which is used in order to significantly reduce the size of a password space for a given user authentication system.

Authentication Schema	Password space reduction based on:
Alphanumeric passwords	Personal and public well known information, which is already remembered by the user
PassFaces	Faces of people who are same race as the user, good looking
Story	Variations in gender preferences
Draw-a-Secret	Symmetry, number of strokes, in grid location
PassPoints	Dismiss large uniform areas, concentrate on regions of interest
Pronounceable Passwords	Phonetic rules of user's language
PassText	Personal information, outlier locations
PassMap	Familiar locations

Table 6.12: Approaches to password space reduction

By analyzing information presented in Table 6.12, we can suggest a way of reducing password space size for any currently existing user authentication mechanism as well as for any similar future system. This is true as long as the system allows the user to select the password as apposed to assigning one randomly selected from the full set of possibilities by the system itself. The general approach for alphanumeric or graphical passwords is to utilize demographic information about the user including but not limited to personal information, race, gender, age, and interests. Such information was already known and remembered by the user prior to the enrolment with the authentication system. So it requires no additional effort to commit to memory and as a result is provided as the password.

In case a user has to select among multiple types of information, to be used as his password, it should be assumed that the user would select the easiest to remember, most symmetric, less complicated object with fewest possible number of components. In a field of many similar items users will select the most distinguished items either in terms of color, shape or some other property.

Users tend to select passwords, which are relatively easy to remember. As we showed in this chapter for any authentication system a diligent hacker can be expected to be successful at taking advantage of the reduced password space. Assigning passwords to users can solve this problem, but this in turn results in forgotten passwords and increased costs of system administration. This motivates as to suggest a move towards biometrics-based user authentication systems as the only solution for secure and user-friendly person identification.

CHAPTER 7 - TRAFFIC ANALYSIS BASED IDENTIFICATION OF NETWORK ATTACKS

"It is a capital mistake to theorize before one has data. Insensibly one begins to twist facts to suit theories, instead of theories to suit facts"

Sir Arthur Conan Doyle (1859 – 1930)

Abstract—*This chapter is devoted to the problem of identification of network attacks via traffic analysis. We show that properly trained neural networks are capable of fast recognition and classification of different attacks. The advantage of the taken approach allows us to demonstrate the superiority of the neural networks over the systems that were created by the winner of the KDD Cups competition and later researchers due to their capability to recognize an attack, to differentiate one attack from another, i.e. classify attacks, and, the most important, to detect new attacks that were not included into the training set. The results obtained through simulations indicate that it is possible to recognize attacks that the intrusion detection system never faced before on an acceptably high level.*

1. INTRODUCTION

One of the most promising areas of research in the area of Intrusion Detection deals with the applications of the Artificial Intelligence (AI) techniques. The most valuable feature of any AI system is the ability to learn automatically according to data inputs and outputs. This characteristic potentially can add more flexibility to Intrusion Detection Systems and remove the necessity to update the database of possible attacks constantly. At this point we talk not just about an Intrusion Detection System (IDS), but about an Intelligent Intrusion Detection System (IIDS), which is capable of creating attack patterns, i.e. learning about new attacks, based on previous experience [326].

Multiple experiments were performed by many research teams to apply AI techniques in intrusion detection. The main goal was to create a system that is capable of detecting different kinds of attacks. The researchers used Defense Advanced Research Project Agency (DARPA) and Knowledge and Data Mining (KDD) Cups benchmark databases for training and detecting attacks in those experiments [326].

Most Intrusion Detection Systems (IDS) perform monitoring of a system by looking for specific "signatures" of behavior. However, using current methods, it is almost impossible to develop comprehensive-enough databases to warn of all attacks. This is for three main reasons. First, these signatures must be hand-coded. Attack signatures that are already known are coded into a database, against which the IDS checks current behavior. Such a system may be very rigid. Second, because there is a theoretically infinite number of methods and variations of attacks, an infinite size database would be required to detect all possible attacks. This, of course, is not feasible. Also, any attack that is not included in the database has the potential to cause great harm. Finally one other problem is that current methods are likely to raise many false alarms. So not only do novel attacks succeed, but legitimate use can actually be discouraged [325].

We investigate the benchmarks provided by the DARPA and KDD [6]. These benchmarks and the experience of prior researchers are utilized to create an IDS that is capable of learning attack behavior and is able to identify new attacks without system update. In other words, we create a flexible system that does not need hand-coded database of signatures, and that can define new attacks based on pattern, not fixed rules provided by a third party [447, 439, 438, 461]. Neural networks are chosen as the means of achieving this goal. The use of neural networks allows us to identify an attack from the training set, also it allows us to identify new attacks, not included into the training set, and perform attack classification [325].

2. ARTIFICIAL INTELLIGENCE TECHNIQUES IN INTRUSION DETECTION

2.1 NEURAL NETWORKS APPROACH

An increasing amount of researchers have investigated the application of neural networks to intrusion detection [466]. If properly designed and implemented, neural networks have the potential to address many of the problems encountered by rule-based approaches [446]. Neural networks were specifically proposed to learn the typical characteristics of system's users and identify statistically significant variations from their established behavior. In order to apply this approach to intrusion detection, we would have to introduce data representing attacks and non-attacks to the neural network to establish automatically coefficients of this network during the training phase. In other words, it will be necessary to collect data representing normal and abnormal behavior and train the neural network on those data. After training is accomplished, a certain number of performance tests with real network traffic and attacks should be conducted.

2.1.1 Supervised Learning Model

Lippmann and Cunningham of MIT Lincoln Laboratory conducted a number of tests employing neural networks for misuse detection [337, 350]. The system was searching for attack-specific keywords in the network traffic. A multi-layer perceptron had been used for detection UNIX host attacks, and attacks to obtain root-privilege on a server. The system was trying to detect the presence of an attack by classifying the inputs into two outputs: normal and attack. The system was able to detect 80% of attacks. The main achievement of this system was its ability to detect old as well as new attacks not included in the training data.

2.1.2 Unsupervised Learning Model

L. Girardin's of UBILAB laboratory performed clustering of network traffic in order to detect attacks. A visual approach was chosen for attack association [361]. Self Organizing Maps (SOM) were employed to project network events on an appropriate 2D-space for visualization, then the network administrator analyzed them. Intrusions were extracted from the view by highlighting divergence from the norm with visual metaphors of network traffic. The main disadvantage of this approach is its need in interpretation of network traffic by an administrator or other authorized person to detect attacks.

Kayacik et al. utilize KDD Cups data set for their experiments. They create three layer of employment [234]: First, individual SOM are associated with each basic Transmission Control Protocol (TCP) feature. This provides a concise summary of the interesting properties of each basic feature, as derived over a suitable temporal horizon. Second, integrates the views provided by the first level SOM into a single view of the problem. At this point, they use the training set labels associated with each pattern to label the respective best matching unit in the second layer. Third, the final layer is built for those neurons, which win for both attack and normal behaviors. This results in third layer SOMs being associated with specific neurons in the second layer. Moreover, the hierarchical nature of the architecture means that the first layer may be trained in parallel and the third layer SOMs are only trained over a small fraction of the data set.

	Normal	DoS	Probe	U2R	R2L
Level 2	92.4	96.5	72.8	22.9	11.3
Level 1	95.4	95.1	64.3	10.0	9.9

Table 7.1: Performance of 2 and 3 layer hierarchy on different categories

The table above describes the detection of attacks by category. In the table below we can see the individual attack detection rates.

Attack Name	Level 2	Level 3
Apache2	90.3%	90.7%
Httptunnel	58.9%	20.9%
Mailbomb	7.8%	6.8%
Mscan	90.2%	60.9%
Named	23.5%	0.0%
Processtable	59.4%	47.6%
Ps	0.0%	0.0%
Saint	79.1%	78.7%
Sendmail	5.9%	11.8%
Snmpgetattack	11.5%	10.3%
Udpstorm	0.0%	0.0%
Xlock	0.0%	0.0%
xsnoop	0.0%	0.0%
Xterm	23.1%	30.8%

Table 7.2: Detection rate of new attacks for 2-layer and 3-layer hierarchy

2.1.3 Hybrid Networks

Several researchers have combined Multi-Layer Perceptron (MLP) and Self-Organizing Map (SOM) in their attempt to create an intrusion detection system. Cannady et al. of Georgia Technical Research Institute and Fox et al. have investigated application of MLP model and SOM for misuse detection [337, 99, 161]. They have used a feed-forward network with back-propagation learning, which contained 4 fully connected layers, 9 input nodes and 2 output nodes (normal and attack). The network has been trained for a certain number of attacks. The network has succeeded in identifying attacks it was trained for.

Bivens believes that Deniel Of Service (DOS) and other network-based attacks leave a faint trace of their presence in the network traffic data. He has designed modular network-based intrusion detection system that analyzes TCP dump data to develop windowed traffic intensity trends, which detects network-based attacks by carefully analyzing this network traffic data and alerting administrators to abnormal traffic trends. It has been shown that network traffic can be efficiently modeled using artificial neural networks [49, 128, 129], therefore MLP was chosen to examine network traffic data. SOM has been used to group network traffic together to present it to the neural network, as SOM have been shown to be effective in novelty detection [470, 173, 234].

The data that they have presented to the neural network consisted of attack-specific keyword counts in network traffic [19]. This system remains a host-based detection system because it looks at the user actions. The neural network was created to analyze program behavior profiles instead of user behavior profiles [171]. This method identifies the normal system behavior of certain programs and compares it to the current system behavior. The author has used DARPA benchmark for the experiments. The prediction rate of the system is 24% - 100%. 100% has been achieved only with one attack in the training set – sshprocesstable [97, 77].

2.2 RULE-BASED APPROACH

Agarwal et al. propose a two-stage general-to-specific framework for learning a rule-based model to learn classifier models on a data set that has widely different class distributions in the training data [27]. They utilized KDD Cups database for training and testing their system. The system was classifying the attacks into 4 main groups: Probing – information gathering, Denial of Service (DOS) – deny legitimate requests to the system, User-to-Root (U2R) – unauthorized access to local super-user or root, Remote-to-Local (R2L) – unauthorized local access from a remote machine.

The system performed very well on detecting Probing and DOS attacks identifying 73.2% and 96.6% respectively. 6.6% of U2R attacks were detected and 10.7% of R2L. False alarms were generated at a level of less than 10% for all attack categories except for U2R – an unacceptably high level of 89.5% false alarm rate was reported for this category.

2.3 DECISION-TREE APPROACH

Levin creates a set of locally optimal decision trees (decision forest) from which optimal subset of trees (sub-forest) is selected for predicting new cases [270]. 10% of KDD Cups database is used for training and testing. Data is randomly sampled from the entire training data set. Multi-class detection approach is used to detect different attack categories in the KDD data set. Just like Agarwal and Joshi [27], Levin tries to classify the data into four main categories: Probing, DOS, U2R, and R2L. The final trees give very high detection rates for all classes including the R2L in the entire training data set. In particular, 84.5% detection rate for Probing, 97.5% for DOS, 11.8% for U2R, and 7.32% for R2L. The following false alarm rates were detected for Probing, DOS, U2R and R2L attack categories respectively - 21.6%, 73.1%, 36.4%, and 1.7%.

2.4 SHARED NEAREST NEIGHBOR AND K-MEANS APPROACH

Ertoz used Shared Nearest Neighbor technique (SNN) that is particularly suited for finding clusters in data of different sizes, density, and shapes, mainly when the data contains large amount of noise and outliers. All attack records are selected from the KDD training and testing data sets with a count of 10,000 records from each attack type: there are a total of 36 attack types from 4 attack categories. Also, 10,000 records were randomly picked from both the training and the testing data sets. In total, around 97,000 records were selected from the entire KDD data set. After removing duplicate KDD records, the data set size was reduced to 45,000 records [152]. The author is utilizing two main clustering algorithms: K-Means, where the number of clusters is equal to 300, and SNN. K-Means performed very well on Probing, DOS, and R2L, detecting 91.8%, 98.75%, and 77.04% respectively. Detection rate for U2R is 5.6%. SNN performed in the following manner: 73.48% for Probing, 77.76% for DOS, 37.82% for U2R, and 68.15% for R2L. False alarms are not discussed by the author.

2.5 PARZEN-WINDOW APPROACH

Yeung et al. propose a novel detection approach using non-parametric density estimation based on Parzen-window estimators with Gaussian kernels to build an intrusion detection system using normal data only. This novel detection approach was employed to detect attack categories in the KDD data set [468]. 30,000 randomly sampled normal records from the KDD training data set were used as training data to estimate the density of the model. 30,000 randomly sampled normal records (also from the KDD training data set) formed the threshold determination set, which had no overlap with the training data set. The results were very high in most cases: 99.17% detection of Probing, 96.71% of DOS, 93.57% of U2R, and 31.17% of R2L. No false alarms information is available. The main advantage of this technique is its capability of classifying the attack, not just detecting it.

2.6 MULTI-CLASSIFIER APPROACH

Multi-classifier combination is a popular approach both in biometrics [408, 407, 406] and intrusion detection. Sabhnani et al. conducted a number of experiments with hybrid systems that contained different approaches for attack classification. KDD Cups database was chosen for the experiments. The attacks were classified into four main groups, as was done by the researchers discussed in prior sections: Probing – information gathering, Denial of Service (DOS) – deny legitimate requests to the system, User-to-Root (U2R) – unauthorized access to local super-user or root, Remote-to-Local (R2L) – unauthorized local access from a remote machine.

They highlight that most researchers employ a single algorithm to detect multiple attack categories with dismal performance in some cases. So, they propose to use a specific detection algorithm that is associated with an attack category for which it is the most promising [361]. Attributes in the KDD datasets had all forms – continuous, discrete, and symbolic, with significantly varying resolution and ranges. Most pattern classification methods are not able to process data in such a format. Hence, preprocessing was required. The preprocessing includes the following steps:

Mapping symbolic-valued attributes to numeric-valued attributes. Symbolic features like protocol_type (3 different symbols), service (70 different symbols), and flag (11 different symbols) were mapped to integer values ranging from 0 to N-1 where N is the number of symbols. Attack names, such as buffer_overflow, were mapped to one of the five classes: Normal was mapped to 0, Probing was mapped to 1, DOS was mapped to 2, U2R was mapped to 3, R2L was mapped to 4 [148].

Scaling: Each of the mapped features was linearly scaled to the range [0.0, 1.0]. Features having smaller integer value ranges like duration [0, 58329], wrong_fragment [0, 3], urgent [0, 14], hot[0, 101], num_failed_logins [0, 5], num_compromised [0, 9], su_attemptes [0, 2], num_root [0, 7468], num_file_creations [0, 100], num_shells [0, 5], num_access_files [0, 9], count [0, 511], srv_count [0, 511], dst_host_count [0, 255], and dst_host_srv_count [0, 255] were also scaled linearly to the range of [0, 1]. Logarithmic scaling (base 10) was applied to two features spanned over a very large integer range, namely src_bytes [0, 1.3 billion] and dts_bytes [0, 1.3 billion], to reduce the range to [0, 9.14]. All other features were either Boolean, like logged_in, having values (0 or 1), or continuous, like diff_srv_rate, in the range of [0, 1]. No scaling was necessary for these attributes.

For the purpose of training different classifier models, all duplicate records were removed from the datasets. The total number of records in the original labeled training dataset is 972, 780 for normal; 41, 102 for Probe; 3,883,370 for DOS; 52 for U2R and 999 for R2L attack classes. All simulations were performed on a multi-user Sun SPARC machine, which has dual microprocessors, ULTRASPARC-II, running at 400 MHz. System clock frequency is equal to 100 MHz., the system had 512 MB of RAM and Solaris 8 operating system.

9 distinct pattern recognition and machine learning algorithms are tested:

- **MLP.** 3 layers of feed forward neural network are implemented. Sigmoid is used as the transfer function and stochastic gradient decent with mean squared error function as the learning algorithm. The network has 41 inputs, 5 outputs, 40 – 80 nodes in the hidden layer, 0.1 – 0.6 learning rate (0.1 the final rate), 500,000 samples in each epoch, and 30 – 150 epochs (60 the final number of epochs).

- **Gaussian classifier (GAU).** This classifier assumes inputs are uncorrelated and distributions for different classes differ only in mean values. It is based on the Bayes decision theorem [145].

- **K-means clustering (K-M).** This algorithm [145] positions K centers in the pattern space such that the total squared error distance between each training pattern and the nearest center is minimized.

- **Nearest cluster algorithm (NEA).** It is a condensed version of K-nearest neighbor clustering algorithm [145]. Input to this algorithm is a set of cluster centers generated from the training data set using standard clustering algorithms like K-means, E & M binary split, and leader algorithm. In this case, the initial clusters were created using the K-means.

- **Incremental Radial Basis Function (IRBF).** Can perform non-linear mapping between input and output vectors similar to RBF and MLP [185].

- **Leader algorithm (LEA).** LEA partitions a set of M records into K disjoint clusters (where M≥K) [188]. First input record forms the leader of the first cluster. Each input record is sequentially compared with current leader clusters. If the distance measure between the current record and all leader records is greater than the threshold, a new cluster is formed with the current record being the cluster leader.

- **Hyper sphere algorithm (HYP).** This algorithm creates decision boundaries using spheres in input feature space [62, 268]. Any pattern that falls within the sphere is classified in the same class as that of the center pattern. Spheres are created using an initial defined radius. Euclidean distance between a pattern and sphere centers is used to test whether a pattern falls in one of the currently defined spheres.

- **Fuzzy ARTMAP (ART).** Adaptive Resonance Theory (ART) mapping algorithm is used for supervised learning of multidimensional data [102]. It uses two ART's – ARTa and ARTb. ARTa maps features into clusters. ARTb maps output categories into clusters. There is a mapping from ARTa clusters to ARTb clusters that is performed during training.

- **C4.5 decision tree (C4.5).** This algorithm was developed by Quinlan [428]. It generates decision trees using an information theoretic methodology. The goal is to construct a decision tree with minimum number of nodes that gives least number of misclassifications on training data. Divide and conquer strategy is utilized in this algorithm. The publicly available pattern classification software tool LNKnet is used to simulate pattern recognition and machine learning models [14]. The C4.5 algorithm is employed to generate decision trees using the software tool described in [12].

In the table below we can see the results of the experiments held by the authors. Here PD represents Probability of Detection, and FAR – False Alarm Rate. They state that the set of pattern recognition and machine learning algorithms tested on the KDD data sets offers an acceptable level of misuse detection performance for only two attack categories - Probing and DOS. On the other hand, all nine classification algorithms fail to demonstrate an acceptable level of detection performance for the remaining two attack categories namely: U2R and R2L. Thus, [361] offers a multi-classifier model: they propose to have sub-classifiers trained using different algorithms for each attack category. They offer the best algorithm for each category: MLP for probing, K-M for DOS, K-M for U2R, GAU for R2L.

		Probe	DoS	U2R	R2L
MLP	*PD*	88.7%	97.2%	13.2%	5.6%
	FAR	0.4%	0.3%	0.1%	0.1%
GAU	*PD*	90.2%	82.4%	22.8%	0.1%
	FAR	11.3%	0.9%	0.5%	0.1%
K-M	*PD*	87.6%	97.3%	29.8%	6.4%
	FAR	2.6%	0.4%	0.4%	0.1%
NEA	*PD*	88.8%	97.1%	2.2%	3.4%
	FAR	0.5%	0.3%	0.1%	0.1%
RBF	*PD*	93.2%	73%	6.1%	5.9%
	FAR	18.8%	0.2%	0.4%	0.3%
LEA	*PD*	83.8%	97.2%	8.3%	1%
	FAR	0.3%	0.3%	0.3%	0.1%
HYP	*PD*	84.8%	97.2%	8.3%	1%
	FAR	0.4%	0.3%	0.1%	0.1%
ART	*PD*	77.2%	97%	6.1%	3.7%
	FAR	0.2%	0.3%	0.1%	0.1%
C4.5	*PD*	80.8%	97%	1.8%	4.6%
	FAR	0.7%	0.3%	0.1%	0.1%

Table 7.3: Multi-classifier results for separate algorithms

The results are depicted in the table below, where we can see the improvement in the performance of the system overall.

		Probe	DoS	U2R	R2L
Multi-Classifier	*Pos Detection*	88.7%	97.3%	29.8%	9.6%
	False Alarms	0.4%	0.4%	0.4%	0.1%

Table 7.4: Multi-classifier results for the final system

3. EXPERIMENTS

In the works we review in some cases accuracy of the classification is as low as 8.4%, which is not acceptable. The main problem with the approach they had chosen was that they used all attacks in the dataset, though many of those attacks did not have enough records for training, as we outlined after the data formatting and optimization took place. If an attack does not have enough presence (IMAP attack had only 12 records), it should not be used for training. Also, they grouped the attacks, what potentially can lead to a misdetection since not all of the attacks in the same group have identical signatures and patterns. Thus, a different approach was chosen to detect and classify attack. The main advantage of this approach was data formatting and the training dataset grouping, which allowed us to increase the accuracy rate up to 100% in some cases, and, the most important advantage, to achieve a high percentage of identification of the attacks that were not included into the training set [327].

The differences between our approach and the approach of other researchers are summarized below. First, we have chosen a different strategy in preprocessing. Before using the dataset, we made a thorough analysis of the given data. We found out that there are a lot of repeated records. It was obvious that some attacks, such as Smurf were taking more than 50% of the whole dataset, and some attacks have only 10 or even less records. To optimize the dataset, to make it appropriate for the training and testing, we wrote a tool that was capable of resolving mentioned above problems and prepare the dataset for the neural networks to use. So, the dataset was optimized: repeated records were removed, dataset was split into multiple files, one attack per file. After the statistics were computed, we chose those attacks that had more representation in the dataset, thus the attacks with insignificant number of records were omitted [327].

The second very important difference was the training set composition. After the records were converted into the neural network readable form, i.e. all values were mapped and scaled into the range [0:1], we created training sets, trying to keep even distribution of the attacks in the set. In other words, if it is important to identify normal behavior from the set of records, the records of the normal behavior have to comprise 50% of the training set. Other 50% should be evenly distributed in the group of attacks [325].

Third, we chose to classify each attack, when others were trying to classify the attacks into different groups. Group classification could potentially lead to confusion, since though the attack belong to the same group, i.e. trying to achieve the same goal, they have different signatures, patterns, and set of actions, thus could be misclassified.

3.1. DATA

To conduct the experiments, it was decided to use the benchmarks of the International Knowledge Discovery and Data Mining group (KDD). These data are based on the benchmark of the Defense Advanced Research Projects Agency (DARPA) that was collected by the Lincoln Laboratory of Massachusetts Institute of Technology in 1998, and was the first initiative to provide designers of intrusion detection systems with a benchmark, on which to evaluate different methodologies [6].

In order to collect these data, a simulation had been made of a factitious military network consisting of three target machines running various operating systems and services. Additional three machines were then used to spoof different IP addresses, thus generating traffic between different IP addresses. Finally, a sniffer was used to record all network traffic using the TCP dump format. The total simulation period was seven weeks.

Normal connections were created to profile those expected in a military network. Attacks fall into one of five categories: User to Root (U2R), Remote to Local (R2L), Denial of Service (DOS), Data, and Probe. Packets information in the TCP dump files were summarized into connections. Specifically, a connection was a sequence of TCP packets starting and ending at some well defined times, between which data flows from a source IP address to a target IP address under some well defined protocol. In 1999 the original TCP dump files were preprocessed for utilization in the IDS benchmark of the International Knowledge Discovery and Data Mining Tools Competitions [195].

The data consists of a number of basic features: duration of the connection, protocol type, such as TCP, UDP or ICMP, service type, such as FTP, HTTP, Telnet, status flag, total bytes sent to destination host, total bytes sent to source host, whether source and destination addresses are the same or not, number of wrong fragments, number of urgent packets. Each record consists of 41 attributes and one target [267, 265]. The target value indicates the attack name. In addition to the above nine basic features, each record is also described in terms of an additional 32 derived features, falling into three categories:

1. Content features: domain knowledge is used to assess the payload of the original TCP packets. This includes features such as the number of failed login attempts.

2. Time-based traffic features: these features are designed to capture properties that mature over a 2 second temporal window. One example of such a feature would be the number of connections to the same host over the 2 second interval.

3. Host-based traffic features: utilize a historical window estimated over the number of connections – in this case 100 – instead of time. Host based features are therefore designed to assess attacks, which span intervals longer than 2 seconds.

In order to perform formatting and optimization of the data, a tool was written that is capable of completing such operations as computing data statistics, data conversion, data optimization, neural network input creation, and other data preprocessing related assignments. Based on the results produced by the Preparation Tool, we made the following classifications: each record consists of 41 fields and one target. The target value indicates the attack name. The data has 4,898,431 records in the dataset. 3,925,650 (80.14%) records represent attacks that fall into one of the five mentioned above categories. Total 22 attacks were identified. 972,781 (19.85%) records of normal behavior were found.

Attributes in the KDD datasets contained multiple types: integers, floats, strings, booleans, with significantly varying resolution and ranges. Most pattern classification methods are not able to process data in such a format. Therefore, preprocessing took place to transform the data into the most optimal format acceptable by the neural networks.

First of all, the dataset was split into multiple files and duplicate records were removed. Each file contained records corresponding to a certain attack or normal behavior. Thus, a library of attacks was created. It was done to achieve an efficient way to format, optimize, and compose custom training and testing datasets. Second, symbolic features like attack name (23 different symbols), protocol type (three different symbols), service (70 different symbols), and flag (11 different symbols) were mapped to integer values ranging from 0 to N-1 where N is the number of symbols. Third, a certain scaling had taken place: each of the mapped features was linearly scaled to the range [0.0, 1.0]. Features having integer value ranges like duration were also scaled linearly to the range of [0, 1]. All other features were either Boolean, like logged_in, having values (0 or 1), or continuous, like diff_srv_rate, in the range of [0, 1]. No scaling was necessary for these attributes.

Attacks with the most number of records were chosen to be in the training set. The following attacks were used to train and to test the neural networks: Smurf, Satan, Neptune, Ipsweep, Back. The following attacks were chosen for the unknown (not trained) set of attacks: Buffer_overflow, Guess_password, Nmap, Teardrop, Warezclient.

3.2 EXPERIMENTS

It was decided to run the experiments in three stages. In stage one, it was important to repeat the experiments of other researchers and have the Neural Networks identify an attack. In stage two the experiment was aimed at a more complicated goal. It was decided to classify the attacks, thus, the Neural Networks had to determine not only the presence of an attack, but the attack itself. Stage three had to repeat the experiments of stage two, but in this stage a set of unknown attacks was added to the testing set. Stage three contains experiments of a higher complexity and interest.

Each Radial Bases Function (RBF) Neural Network had 41 inputs, corresponding to each attribute in the dataset, two outputs for attack detection (the first output for the presence of an attack – "yes", the second output for the normal behavior – "no"), or six outputs for attack classification (five outputs for the attacks, and the sixth output for the normal behavior), three layers (input, hidden, and output). The training set consisted of 4000 records. The attack and the normal behavior records were evenly distributed in the training set.

The parameters of the Multiple Layer Perceptron (MLP) NN were: similar to those of RBF NN, but with some differences including: the hidden layer had 20 nodes, alpha = 0.7, beta = 0.8, "tansig" function is used in the input layer node, "purelin" in the hidden and output layer nodes, 50 epochs. The training set consisted of 4000 records. The attack and the normal behavior records were evenly distributed in the training set.

3.3 RESULTS

The first stage of the experiments consisted of 2 phases. First, only one attack was used in the training set. The distribution of an attack and normal records was 50% - 50%. Table 7.5 represents the results of these experiments. As it is shown, the accuracy of positive recognition is very high for both Neural Networks. All of the attacks have more than 90% recognition. Most of them are very close to 100%, what is a very good and expected result.

Attack Name	RBF Accuracy	RBF False Alarms	MLP Accuracy	MLP False Alarms
Smurf	100%	0%	99.5%	0%
Neptune	100%	0%	100%	0%
Satan	91%	7%	97.2%	2%
IP Sweep	99.5%	0%	99.9%	0%
Back	100%	0%	100%	0%

Table 7.5: One attack dataset results

For the second phase of the first stage of the experiments, five different attacks were used in the training set. Normal behavior records was considered as an attack, thus total of six attacks were used in this stage. In order to proceed to the next level of the experiments, attack classification, it was important to prove that the attacks are distinguishable. Therefore, six different experiments were held to prove this idea. 50% of the training set consisted of the concentrated attack, i.e. the attack that had to be differentiated from the others. Other 50% were evenly distributed between other attacks, i.e. 10% per attack. For example, normal behavior records needed to be defined. 50% of the training set for this assignment consisted of the records of normal behavior and other 50% contained records of Smurf, Neptune, Satan, IP Sweep, and Back attacks. All records were in random order.

Table 7.6 demonstrates the results of this experiment. As shown in the table, the accuracy for differentiating the attacks is quite high for both Neural Networks. The lowest accuracy is 91% for Satan and the highest is 100% for Smurf, Neptune, and Back. These results let us make a conclusion that attacks can be differentiated, thus classified.

Attack Name	RBF Accuracy	RBF False Alarms	MLP Accuracy	MLP False Alarms
Smurf	100%	0%	99.5%	0%
Neptune	100%	0%	100%	0%
Satan	91%	7%	97.2%	2%
IP Sweep	99.5%	0%	99.9%	0%
Back	100%	0%	100%	0%
Normal	98.0%	1%	96.8%	2%

Table 7.6: Fife attack dataset results

For the second stage of the experiments neural networks with six outputs were used. At this level there was an attempt to create an intrusion detection system that is capable of classifying the attacks. A dataset of five attacks and normal behavior records were used.The attacks were evenly distributed in the dataset.

Table 7.7 demonstrates the result of this experiment. As we can see the accuracy of classifying attacks is 93.2% using RBF Neural Network and 92.2% using MLP Neural Network. The results were very close and the difference is statistically insignificant. In most cases the Networks managed to classify an attack correctly. The false alarm rate (false positive) is very low in both cases, missed attacks rate (false negative) is not high either, and the misidentified attacks rate (misclassification of the attacks) is 5%-6%. Overall, it is possible to conclude that both neural networks are capable of classifying the attacks.

	Accuracy	False Alarms	Missed Attacks	Mis-identified Attacks
RBF	93.2%	0.8%	0.6%	5.4%
MLP	92.2%	0%	2.1%	5.7%

Table 7.7: Attack classification

For the final stage of the experiments we used the trained NN from the second stage. The networks were trained to classify the following attacks: Smurf, Neptune, Satan, IP Sweep, Back, and Normal behavior records. At this point we proceeded with the most interesting and exciting phase of the experiments – untrained (unknown) attack identification.

As it was mentioned earlier, five attacks were chosen to be used for this purpose: Buffer Overflow, Guess Password, NMap, Teardrop, and Warezclient. Datasets of these attacks were sent into the trained neural networks.

Table 7.8 demonstrates the results: RBF neural network managed to identify the unknown attacks as one of the trained attacks in most cases. As for the MLP neural network, it succeeded only with NMap and Guess Password attacks. In other cases it identified the attacks as normal behavior. Thus, RBF displayed capability to identifying unknown attacks while MLP failed in some cases.

Attack Name	MLP	RBF
Buffer Overflow	53.3%	96.6%
Guess Password	96.2%	100%
NMap	99.5%	100%
Teardrop	1%	84.9%
Warezclient	8%	94.3%

Table 7.8: Unknown attack identification

The winner of the last KDD intrusion detection competition Pfahringer, used C5 decision trees, the second-place performance was achieved by Levin using Kernel Miner tool, and the third-place contestants, Miheev et al. used a decision tree based expert system [11]. Also, we note the results of the most recent research made by Sabhnani et al. who used a multi classifier model to achieve even better results than the winner of the KDD Cups contest [361].

Table 7.9 compares the mentioned above results. As we can see, in some cases accuracy of the classification is as low as 8.4%, which is not acceptable. The main problem with the approach they had chosen was that they used all attacks in the dataset, though many of those attacks did not have enough records for training, as we outlined after the data formatting and optimization took place. If an attack does not have enough presence (IMAP attack had only 12 records), it should not be used for training.

Also, they grouped the attacks, what potentially can lead to a misdetection since not all of the attacks in the same group have identical signatures and patterns. Thus, a different approach was chosen to detect and classify attack. The main advantage of this approach was data formatting and the training dataset grouping, which allowed us to increase the accuracy rate up to 100% in some cases, and to achieve a high percentage of identification of the attacks that were not included into the training set.

		Probe	**DoS**	**U2R**	**R2L**
KDD Cup Winner	*Accuracy*	83.3%	97.1%	13.2%	8.4%
	False Alarms	0.6%	0.3%	0.1%	0.1%
KDD Cup RunnerUp	*Accuracy*	83.3%	97.1%	13.2%	8.4%
	False Alarms	0.6%	0.3%	0.1%	0.1%
Multi-Classifier	*Accuracy*	88.7%	97.3%	29.8%	9.6%
	False Alarms	0.4%	0.4%	0.4%	0.1%

Table 7.9: Results comparison

4. CONCLUSIONS

Many modern commercially used intrusion detection systems employ the techniques of expert systems that require constant updates from the vendors. This design makes the IDS static, inflexible, and not capable of detecting new attacks without new patches. To improve the security, a lot of researchers put efforts to utilize artificial intelligence techniques in the area of intrusion detection, in order to create systems capable of detecting unknown attacks, and learning new attack signatures by themselves.

Benchmarks were created to standardize and compare the work of different investigators of this problem. Competitions were held to attract the attention of new researchers. In most cases decision-making trees were used. After extensive study, we decided to come up with a unique solution, and approached the problem with a new dataset formatting and optimization technique.

A library of attacks was created. This library was based on the benchmark provided by the MIT Lincoln Lab that was optimized by the KDD Cups. After the data was carefully formatted and optimized, it was decided to use and compare two different neural networks in attack detection and classification. Neural networks were chosen due to their abilities to learn and classify. Trained neural networks can make decisions quickly, making it possible to use them in real-time detection.

Both types of neural networks managed to perform well on the known set of attacks, i.e. attacks that they were trained to identify and classify. After new attacks were added to the testing set, i.e. attacks that were not included into the training set, Radial Basis Function Neural Network performed significantly better than Multiple Layer Perceptron with the detection rate between 80% and 100%, and the false alarm rate not greater than 2%.

When we compared these results to the results of previous work, it was notable that the chosen technique had its advantages. First of all, we managed to correctly detect the attacks. Second, classification of the trained attacks was successful with the rate of 90-100%. Third, and the most important, we were able to detect new unknown attacks, which were not included into the training set. The accuracy of detecting new unknown attacks was between 80% and 100%.

After performing our experiments we concluded that with appropriate data formatting, optimization, and dataset composition, neural networks display very good performance and potential in detecting and classifying trained attacks, as well as new unknown attacks that were not included into the training set.

CHAPTER 8 - BEHAVIORAL BIOMETRICS – FUTURE DIRECTIONS

"Now this is not the end. It is not even the beginning of the end. But it is, perhaps, the end of the beginning"

Sir Winston Churchill (1874 - 1965)

Abstract—*This exploratory chapter begins with an overview of a multidisciplinary problem of behavior modeling. It looks at many possible applications of such technology and proposes some novel directions for future research. From the security point of view the chapter proposes and explores some novel behavioral biometrics and research paths as well as some universal descriptors of behavior in general. It concludes with an analysis of how behavior can be influenced by the environment in particular location of the individual engaging in the behavior.*

1. INTRODUCTION

It is often the case in the scientific discovery process that multiple sub-fields of science study the same concept simultaneously but are not aware of the contributions made in the other fields to what essentially is the same problem. Multiple disciplines use different motivation for their research as well as create unique vocabulary to deal with the problem at hand. A lot of progress in finding a solution to such a problem can be made by realizing similarity of research goals and making scientists realize the wealth of available techniques from other fields which may be used with little to no modification for solving a problem at hand. We start by presenting just such a problem addressed by many fields, which are relatively unaware of each other, but all attempt to model human behavior [442].

- **User Profiling** – is studied by researchers in the field of Intrusion Detection. It consists of observing someone interacting with a computer, creating a model of such behavior and using it as a template for what is considered a normal behavior for that particular user. If the behavior of supposedly the same user is significantly different we can speculate that perhaps it is a different user masquerading as the user whose profile is stored in our security system as a template.

- **User Modeling** – is studied for marketing and customization purposes. It aims at creating a representation of the user for the purpose of customizing products and service to better suite the user. For example software can be made to only display options which are in the field of interest of this particular user making it easier for him to interact with an otherwise very complicated piece of software.

- **Opponent Modeling** – is related to the field of Game Theory and studies different models for understanding and predicting behavior of players in different games [193, 101, 392]. While for many games such as chess it is sufficient for victory to play the best possible strategy and ignore the unique behavior of your opponent in many other games such as poker it is not. Having a well performing prediction model of your opponent's behavior can give you an edge necessary to defeat him in an otherwise equal game [263].

- **Behavioral Biometrics** – are a subset of biometrics, which are generally studied by security system developers. Behavioral biometrics are measurable properties of person's actions which can be used to verify user's identity. An example of a popular behavioral biometric is the way a person types on a keyboard; it has been definitively shown that it is unique enough to provide reliable person verification [182].

- **Criminal Profiling** – as done by police and FBI investigators is the practice of trying to determine personality and identity of an individual who has committed a crime based on the behavior, which was exhibited during the criminal act.

- **Jury Profiling** – is a technique used by lawyers to attempt to predict how a particular potential juror will vote with respect to the verdict based on juror's current behavior, answers to a questioner and overall physical and psychological appearance of the juror.

While the researchers faced with the above problems represent relatively unrelated disciplines they are all essentially trying to achieve the same exact goals. They want to be able to do the following:

- By analyzing past and current actions create an accurate model of individual human's behavior capable of predicting future actions based on a given situation and environmental factors.

- Given a description of behavior either identify an individual likely to conduct himself in such manner or to verify if a given individual is likely to behave in such a way.

Basically in its most generalized form the problem boils down to a mapping from the set of behaviors to individuals and vise versa. However we can ask if it is possible to create more complicated mappings between personality and behavior.

Given occurrence of some behavior by an individual can we predict happening of another smilingly unrelated behavior by the same individual? It is obvious that in the case of related behaviors the answer is definitely yes, for example someone who buys a first and second album by a famous rap artist is likely to also purchase a third one. But in the case of completely unrelated behaviors we don't have any strong evidence supporting or disproving possibility of such correspondence. For example do people who collect stamps are also more likely to enjoy horseback riding?

Some research suggests that there is a connection between one set of behaviors and another. Rentfrow et al. in the Journal of Personality and Social Psychology report that they found a connection between person's musical preferences and other unrelated social behaviors [435]. The most famous example from the field of data mining tells us that people who buy diapers also tend to buy beer in the same trip to the store. Clearly this is a very interesting and beneficial area of research. The possible applications for cross-behavioral prediction are numerous. Perhaps it is possible to make judgments about intelligence or health of an individual from something as benign as routine computer interaction. Maybe we can learn to judge suitability of a potential mate from table manners or find a reliable business partner by watching a person park his car.

Another interesting question to ask is: if two different individuals have similar behavioral profiles and individual A performs a novel behavior is it likely that individual B will also perform the same behavior in the near future. Intuitively it seems very plausible, for example, if two different people recently got married and left on a honeymoon we can expect that seeing one of them buy baby related items may allow us to predict similar purchases by the other in the nearest future. Obviously in this contrived example we had alternative ways of figuring this out.

It would seem desirable to have a single discipline devoted to solving such an important problem for many fields, but in reality a number of somewhat different fields all attempt to work on it to some degree, not mentioning the fields listed above we have:

- **Behaviormetrics** – which studies human behavior on the basis of statistics and information technology. Methodology in behavioral sciences is studied and mathematical or statistical models for understanding human behavior are developed [471].

- **Behavioral Sciences** – "essentially investigates the decision processes and communication strategies within and between organisms in a social system. BS encompasses all the disciplines that explore the behavior and strategies within and between organisms in the natural world. It involves the systematic analysis and investigation of humans and animal behavior, through controlled and naturalistic experimental observations and rigorous formulations" [2].

Both of which can be put under a more general umbrella of science of psychology defined as: "scientific study of human behavior, mental processes, and how they are affected and/or affect an individuals or group's physical state, mental state, and external environment. It's goal is to describe, understand, predict, and modify behavior" [147].

We propose attacking the given problem from the point of view of computer science in general and Intrusion Detection Systems (IDS) and biometrics research in particular. Our choice is motivated by the fact that IDS and biometrics has tools and methodologies necessary for solving the problem. IDS would benefit from all aspects of such research and already has a proven track record in the field. The rest of this chapter analyzes potential future directions of research in analyzing peculiarities of human behavior.

2. BIOMETRICS

There are two types of biometrics: Physical Biometrics (PB) and Behavioral Biometrics (BB) also known as Kinetics [4]. PB are defined as: biological properties of an individual that uniquely determine identity. BB are defined as: "characteristic traits exhibited by a person that can determine identity" in other words they attempt to quantify the unique actions that people perform [187]. Physical biometrics are typically considered to be more reliable and so may be used for user identification or verification. Behavioral biometrics are considered less reliable and so are only used for verification, but it might be possible to achieve certain levels of accuracy even in recognition applications particularly by utilizing multi-modal behavioral biometrics. Behavioral biometrics also have some advantages over Physical biometrics, such as:

- Collection of data for BB is far less intrusive, often unnoticeable by the person being profiled.

- Behavioral biometrics tend to raise fewer privacy concerns since the behavior is already publicly observable [9].

- Based on the needs of the application behavioral measurements can be collected to accommodate different security thresholds. The longer we observe a particular behavior the more accurate description of it we can generate [107] .

- BB are also often less expensive to implement since they require less or none of specialized hardware [142].

2.1. BEHAVIORAL BIOMETRICS

2.1.1. Software Interaction-Based Behavioral biometrics

A large number of Behavioral Biometrics is currently under investigation including: Voice, Signature, Keystroke dynamics, Handwriting, Lip motion, Gait, Gesture and grip [4]. Behavioral biometrics can be subdivided into a number of groups, one such group being comprised of behaviors related to the manipulation of computer software. This particular type is also known as user profiling based. Up to this point a lot of research in behavioral biometrics concentrated on a very low level behavior of the users such as keystroke dynamics and mouse movements which are used to interact with a computer. While relatively accurate, those behavioral biometrics only concentrate on manifestations of behavior dependent on physical abilities of an individual and completely ignore higher level intentional behaviors, which may provide superior descriptors for successfully verifying identity of human beings.

User interaction with almost every type of software can be used to generate a personalized behavioral signature capable of verifying user's identity. While some research in that area has been done, particularly with command line interfaces [296, 365] and more recently with point and click interfaces [175] much more can be accomplished. Usually low-level side effects of user activity are all that is taken to generate a user profile. For example one study concentrated on things like number of open windows, time between new windows and number of words in a window title [175]. As the technology advances it may become possible to use higher-level behaviors to generate more accurate user profiles:

- **OS interaction behavior:** A profile consists of OS specific behaviors of the user. Almost every task in a modern OS can be accomplished with multiple equally well performing approaches. So a user's choice of doing some task may constitute a single data point in the behavioral signature. For example using a desktop icon to start an application as apposed to going through the Start button in the MS

Windows environment. Dozens if not hundreds of similar choices provide a wealth of behavioral information sufficient to verify if the same user is interacting with the OS.

- **Web browsing behavior:** Just as unique as the OS manipulation behavior can be the set of actions user takes to work with a network such as Internet. The choice of web browser, search engine, collection of often-visited sites and other similar web related choices could be a great personal identifier. Online searching behavior can be a particularly telling descriptor since the choice of keywords used, topics of searching and skill necessary to construct complicated logical predicates say a lot about who the person is.

- **Email checking – sending behavior:** In addition to the different people we all chose to communicate with via email, we all have unique ways of composing emails. Even a simple task of replying to an email can be done very differently. Some people choose to include the original message in the response there is others insist on deleting it. Some add a complicated personalized signature to the end of the message while others simply send "regards". The number of emails sent and received also greatly varies. Many other personal choices can also be considered such as how a person reads his new messages. Some people tend to read them all first and choose to reply to some at a later time, while others always immediately reply to a new message not wishing to keep the sender waiting for a response.

- **Word processing behavior:** There is a million different ways to format a document. Choices of fonts, styles, paragraph structure and so on can be as unique as the users who compose those documents. In addition a great amount of additional information can be collected about the actual writing of the individual such as common topic, vocabulary size, common spelling and grammatical errors.

- **Media interaction behavior:** Modern computers serve as DVD players, stereo systems, photo albums and art galleries to name just some media related applications. How a user organizes a play list of songs, speed with which he looks through a photo album and which news feeds he likes to listen too can be used to tell different users a part.

- **Photo editing behavior:** An operation of a complicated photo processing software such as Photoshop requires a significant level of skill. Just like with OS or word processors no two users will perform many complicated tasks exactly the same way. Since many different images require similar processing we can quickly collect enough data to start verifying user identities in the creative environments such as provided by image processing software.

- **Any other software:** An attentive reader can clearly notice a pattern in the above behavioral biometrics related to software use. All software provides many ways and options for accomplishing similar tasks. The more complicated a piece of software is the more unique will be a behavioral signature generated by the user of the said piece of software. This might be particularly true in security sensitive domains of power management companies and intelligence agency's databases where verifying user's identity is a task second in importance only to the primary function of the software.

2.1.2. Novel Behavioral Biometrics from Video Surveillance

Big brother is watching you. The surveillance cameras are no longer limited to convenience stores. Banks, libraries, airports, factories and even street corners are under constant observation not to mention prisons, police stations, and government buildings. For example in London there are at least 500,000 cameras in the city, and one study showed that in a single day a person could expect to be filmed 300 times [223]. With such a wealth of data it is only logical that we will try to use this information to find, recognize, identify and verify people.

Obviously the best approach to doing so is via face recognition but since it is not always possible, as in the cases there no clear face shot is available, alternative biometric solutions can be exploited. Gait has been one such alternative being researched at multiple centers around the world. We propose a number of behavior-based biometrics, which can be extracted from surveillance videos and analyzed without inconveniencing even a single person with document checks, body searches and similar extreme measures.

Today the processing necessary to obtain desired information may be well beyond capabilities of our technology, but the capabilities of biometric science are quickly growing and it is entirely possible to have prototypes of such technologies available in a few years and working systems in a decade or so. In any case, the first step is to identify what technology is desirable to have before any such technology begins its way from research lab to the deployment in the field, and this is precisely this first step this chapter aims at taking.

- **Eating and drinking behavior:** Since many restaurants and café houses with outside sitting enjoy the security provided by surveillance cameras it is possible to considers person's eating habits as a behavioral biometric. The type of a diet a person follows such as vegetarian, vegan, kosher, or Atkins is a good personal descriptor. How a person eats, how they hold a fork, use a napkin, cut their stake, all that can be useful for identification purposes. What sides they choose with their meal, do they use a lot of salt, pepper or hot sauce all such information can add uniqueness to their behavioral signature. Additionally we can consider interaction with the restaurant staff such as ordering and tipping habits.

- **Interaction with electronics:** In our everyday life we are constantly using different electronic devices. We get money from ATMs, talk on our cell phones, watch TV or listen to radio, in all such situations we are very particular about just how we interact with the above-mentioned devices. If we take cell phones as an example some people prefer to use speakerphone while others go with a hands free ear-set. We all use different dialing fingers, hold phone at a different angle, and keep the phone in various locations in or on our wardrobe. Similar observations can be made about all other interactions with electronics, from TV channel flipping habits to notebook carrying style.

- **Shopping habits**: Shopping habits of people have long been subject to intense data mining scrutiny in hopes of finding ways to improve sales and increase success of special promotions. For a behavioral profile we can look at what form of payment a person uses. Do they go with a shopping cart or a basket, which order do the take scanning shelves of different products, not to mention which products they select and how those products can be used to better characterize them.

- **Exercise routine**: Lots of people try to stay lean and healthy by going to the gym. Gyms provide an enormous amount of personal choices for the individual. Hundreds of different machines each one with unique settings options, swimming pools, saunas, and locker rooms. A security system can keep track of the times of attendance, duration of exercise, machines and weights used, and type of exercises performed.

- **Dress and appearance choices**: Many people have a very unique dress style, often with a particular piece of attire so unique it is sufficient to immediately identify them. Even though the daily choice of wardrobe changes the style frequently remains the same. Some people like loose hanging T-shirts, some prefer cloths so tight they have hard time putting it on. Hats, high heels, scarf, jewelry, hairstyles all allow us to show our personality and at the same time to successfully profile us.

- **Other Behaviors**: Any skill behavior, any preference or anything else which makes us who we are can be used as a behavioral descriptor. The list below is not all-inclusive and is only meant to spark ideas for novel research directions and groundbreaking projects. Can a behavior biometric be developed around: Working habits, Social behavior (social contacts, hand shaking), Knowledge (what types of information this person knows about), Sense of humor (how a person laughs), Temper (aggressive, passive), Intelligence (capacity to learn and remember, behavior in a classroom environment), Interests (books, hobbies), Athletic ability (fighting style, dancing style, swimming style), Talents (drawing, singing, playing musical instruments), Likes / dislikes (rap music, tanning), Sexual preferences and physical preference for others, Strategy for using tools, Grooming and hygiene habits, Picture taking(picture posing and acting), Public speaking(presenting mannerisms), Psychological disorders (paranoia, schizophrenia), Credit cards(use and payment pattern), Seat choice(on a plain or movie theater), Investing(stocks, bank account preferences), Interaction with animals(pets).

3. GENERAL PROPERTIES OF BEHAVIOR

While the set of all possible behaviors is truly infinite it might be possible to find some measurable properties of behavior, which can be found in all behaviors and correspond well between different behaviors in the same individual. This would be extremely useful in Multi-modal Behavioral Biometrics (MBB) in which multiple different behaviors are used together to create a single profile. Examples of MBB include combining mouse movement data with keyboard dynamics or voice with lip motion and typically significantly increase accuracy of the system. Ideally at the same time those cross-behavioral property measurements will be somewhat different between different individuals making it easier to tell different people apart. Some possible cross-behavioral properties are presented below:

- **Speed** – how fast a behavior is performed. Examples may include typing speed and number of words spoken per minute.

- **Correctness** – number of mistakes as compared to the desired behavior in a given situation. For example number of mistyped characters or slips of the tongue.

- **Redundancy** – useless repetitiveness of the same behavior per time period. For example saying same thing twice.

- **Consistency** – a statistical measurement of how similar this person's behavior is from one data taking section to the other. Some people are more predictable than others and tend to follow the same routine more precisely.

- **Rule obedience** – some people believe that rules are made to be broken. They park next to fire hydrants, cheat on exams, take 10 items to a 7 or less items cash register and abuse the proper rules of spoken language. The opposite of that behavior is strict following of the rules to the point of absurdity, such as putting a seatbelt on to sit in a parked car. In any case people of those two types are relatively consistent in their rule obedience across different behaviors.

4. ENVIRONMENT AND BEHAVIOR

One of the problems with behavioral biometrics is that human behavior itself is not perfectly repetitive. People act differently based on their current mood, illness, sleep deprivation, drugs, stress, conflict, hunger, previous events and surrounding environment. For example, a person who did not get enough sleep may act irritated, shout a lot and be sloppy at performing his work duties. While fully understanding human emotions may be well beyond capability of modern computers it might be possible to incorporate the effects of the environment into the behavioral model.

The main component of the environment is the geo-spatial location of the individual. The same person will act very differently if they are in privacy of their home or at a public event. In terms of computer networks we can observe that a person who is connecting to the network from his home computer may perform different actions as compared to the times he was accessing the network from his work computer. This leads us to the following thesis: Location influences behavior. We are not claiming that knowing individual's location is sufficient condition for predicting his or her behavior, but we propose that it is one of the factors knowing which may increase the accuracy of behavior prediction.

As more and more computers and mobile devices such as cell phones come equipped with GPS (Global Positioning System) chips identifying location of an individual will become trivial. For now individual's location can be obtained by looking up IP address information for the computer from which individual is accessing the network.

Continuing with our previous example of a person accessing a network from different locations and assuming that the network in question is Internet we can predict that if an individual is accessing Internet from his home computer he will be more likely to check the schedule of movies at a local theater playing within the next hour than to perform a search for suppliers of aluminum tubing (assuming he works in the acquisitions department). So knowing the geo-spatial location of an individual our behavior prediction model can be fine-tuned to produce much better results. While the above example is trivial, it might be possible to anticipate some changes in behavior caused by any number of factors and include such changes in our dynamic personal behavior model.

However good our algorithms are it is still very possible for a behavior based biometric to generate a number of false alarms. This can be seen as a significant shortcoming, but can also be viewed as beneficial. Suppose the system triggers an alarm for an abnormal behavior pattern, but quick investigation positively verifies individual's identity. So now we can conclude that for some reason the individual is not acting like himself. This information can be beneficial for example in the domain of games, more specifically Poker, there knowing that a very strong player is not using his usual superior strategy may be very valuable. It is possible the player in question is on *tilt* (temporary psychological instability) and so will likely make some bad decisions which a good player can take advantage of. A similar example in workplace may indicate that an individual is out of it, and is likely to be performing a substandard level work and so it might benefit the company to temporarily remove that employee from his position, maybe sending him on a well-needed vocation.

6. CONCLUSIONS AND FUTURE DIRECTIONS

Fields as diverse as biometrics, marketing, game theory, security and law enforcement all can greatly benefit from accurate modeling of human behavior. The aim of this exploratory chapter was to show that the problem at hand is not unique to any given field and that a solution found once might benefit many industries without a need for rediscovering it for each sub-field.

General introduction to the field of biometrics and more particularly behavioral biometrics is given alongside the benefits of this non-intrusive approach. An overview of possible software based behavioral biometrics was given followed by a large exploratory section on potential future lines of research in video surveillance based behavioral biometrics. We proposed and explored some novel behavioral biometrics and research paths as well as some universal descriptors of behavior in general. It was followed with an analysis of how behavior can be influenced by the environment in particular location of the individual engaging in the behavior.

As our research evolved many potentially fruitful lines of research worth investigating were determined including:

- Increasing accuracy of intrusion detection systems by employing multi-behavioral biometrics for example combining keyboard dynamics with mouse dynamics and command line lexicon.

- It may be valuable for multi-modal behavioral biometrics researchers to study universal behavioral descriptors such as speed and correctness.

- Implementing a combination physical-behavioral biometric system.

- Experimenting with different behaviors in context of intelligent agent verification and recognition.

- Investigating possibility that people who share same personality traits may have correlations in behavior.

- Much more could be done to better understand precisely how environmental factors, such as location, influence human behavior.

- Research possibility of predicting changes in behavior if changes in the environment are known.

- Handling behavioral drift by utilizing short term and long term behavioral profiles.

- Using data collected from a notebook's touch-pad to develop novel user verification technology similar to mouse dynamics in approach.

Future of behavioral research looks very bright. The next decade will bring us technologies providing unprecedented level of security, product customization, social compatibility and work efficiency. Ideas presented in the section on novel behavioral biometrics provide a wealth of opportunities for interesting research and development. A great side effect of such research would be general greater understanding of human behavior, personality and perhaps human mind itself.

CHAPTER 9 - BIBLIOGRAPHY

For several years we have collected references relating to intrusion detection, behavioral biometrics, cheating in games, and overall topic of computer security. The bibliography contains over 400 references spanning years from 1974 to 2007. We have undoubtedly forgotten some important citations or made errors in the included ones, but we plan on keeping this bibliography updated and will include any corrections sent in by our readers. Included references are not classified or annotated, but we hope this will not prevent this bibliography from being useful to researchers in the field.

[1]   -.   -,   *ASCII   art,*   *Wikipedia,*   Available   at: http://en.wikipedia.org/wiki/Ascii_Art, Retrieved October 21, 2005.

[2]   -.   -,   *Behavioural   sciences,*   *Available   at:* *http://en.wikipedia.org/wiki/Behavioral_sciences,* Retrieved October 6, 2005.

[3]   -.   -,   *Biopassword,*   Available   at: http://www.biopassword.com/bp2/welcome.asp, Retrieved October 24, 2005.

[4]   -.   -,   *Caslon-Analytics,*   *Available   at:* *http://www.caslon.com.au/biometricsnote6.htm,* Retrieved October 2, 2005.

[5]   -. -, *Cheating at Online Poker? A Detailed Analysis, Play No Evil Game Security,*   Available   at: http://www.playnoevil.com/serendipity/index.php?/archives/772-Cheating-at-Online-Poker-A-Detailed-Analysis.html, September 11, 2006.

[6]   -. -, *DARPA, Intrusion Detection Evaluation, MIT Lincoln Laboratory,* Available at: http://www.ll.mit.edu/ist/ideval, 1998.

[7]   -. -, *Encyberpedia US Map with Capitals*, Available at: http://www.encyberpedia.com/cities.htm, Retrieved October 23, 2005.

[8]   -.   -, *FAQ, BioPrivacy Initiative*, Available at: http://www.bioprivacy.org/faqmain.htm, Retrieved July 22, 2005.

[9]   -. -, *FAQ's and Definitions, International Biometric Group, LLC*, Available at: http://www.bioprivacy.org/bioprivacy_text.htm, Retrieved October 2, 2005.

[10]   -. -, *The History of ASCII (Text) Art*, Available at: http://www.acid.org/info/mirror/jgs/history.html#typography,   Retrieved October 21, 2005.

[11]   -. -, *http://www-cse.ucsd.edu/users/elkan/clresults.html*, KDD Cups 99 - Intrusion Detection Contest (1999).

[12]   -. -, *http://www.rulequest.com, C4.5*, 2004.

[13]   -.   -, *The Journey System, Mindtools*, Available at: http://www.mindtools.com/pages/article/newTIM_05.htm,   Retrieved October 22, 2005.

[14]   -. -, *LNKnet*, Available at: http://www.ll.mit.edu/IST/lnknet/index.html, 2004.

[15]   -.   -, *Online Cheating*, Available at: http://www.tips4poker.com/content/online_poker_cheating.html, Retrieved November 14, 2006.

[16]   -.   -, *PicturePINs, Pointsec*, Available at: http://www.pointsec.com/news/download/Pointsec_PPC_2.0_POP_PA1.pd f, November 2002.

[17]   -. -, *Player id, age verification and border control technology forum, Nevada Interactive Gaming Task Force*, Available at: http://www.nevadaigtf.org/TechnologyForum.html., Retrieved October 23, 2005.

[18] -. -, *Pokerprophecy* Available at: http://www.pokerprophecy.com, Retrieved September 26, 2006.

[19] -. -, *Practical Overview: Intrusion Detection Systems, Security*, Available at: http://www.wlcg.com/uploadedfiles/IntrusionDetectionGuide3.pdf, 2005.

[20] -. -, *The Science Behind Passfaces, Real User Corporation*, Available at: http://www.realuser.com/, June 2004.

[21] -. -, *Stats and Analysis, Poker-edge.com*, Available at: http://www.poker-edge.com/stats.php, Retrieved June 7, 2006.

[22] -. -, *TV That Watches You: The Prying Eyes of Interactive Television A Report by the Center for Digital Democracy*, Available at: www.democraticmedia.org/privacyreport.pdf, June 2001.

[23] -. -, *Windholdem Detection Avoidance*, Available at: http://www.winholdem.net/antidetect.html, Retrieved November 26, 2006.

[24] A. Abbas, Abdulmotaleb, E. Saddik and A. Miri, *A State of the Art Security Taxonomy of Internet Security: Threats and Countermeasures*, Int'l Trans. Computer Science and Engineering, 19 (2005), pp. 27-36.

[25] E. F. Aboufadel, J. Olsen and J. Windle, *Breaking the Holiday Inn Priority Club CAPTCHA*, *The College Mathematics Journal*, March 2005.

[26] A. Adler, R. Youmaran and S. Loyka, *Towards a Measure of Biometric Information*, Available at: http://www.sce.carleton.ca/faculty/adler/publications/2006/youmaran-ccece2006-biometric-entropy.pdf, Retrieved August 2, 2006.

[27] R. Agarwal and M. Joshi, *PNrule: A New Framework for Learning Classifier Models in Data Mining*, Technical Report TR 00-015 (2000).

[28]   A. A. E. Ahmed and I. Traore, *Anomaly Intrusion Detection based on Biometrics*, *Workshop on Information Assurance*, United States Military Academy, West Point, NY, June 2005.

[29]   A. A. E. Ahmed and I. Traore, *Detecting Computer Intrusions Using Behavioral Biometrics*, *Third Annual Conference on Privacy, Security and Trust*, St. Andrews, New Brunswick, Canada, October, 2005.

[30]   L. v. Ahn, *Utilizing the Power of Human Cycles*, *Thesis Proposal. Carnegie Mellon University*, May 2004.

[31]   L. v. Ahn, M. Blum, N. Hopper and J. Langford, *CAPTCHA: Using Hard AI Problems for Security*, *In Eurocrypt*, 2003.

[32]   L. v. Ahn, M. Blum and J. Langford, *How Lazy Cryptographers do AI*, *In Communications of the ACM*, Feb. 2004.

[33]   U. Aickelin, J. Greensmith and J. Twycross, *Immune system approaches to intrusion detection - a review*, in G. Nicosia, ed., *Proc. of the Third International Conference on Artificial Immune Systems Number 3239 in Lecture Notes in Computer Science*, Springer, 2004, pp. 316--329.

[34]   S. Al-Zubi, A. Brömme and K. Tönnies, *Using an Active Shape Structural Model for Biometric Sketch Recognition*, *In Proceedings of DAGM*, Magdeburg, Germany, 10.-12. September 2003, pp. 187-195.

[35]   H. Albag, *Network & Agent Based Intrusion Detection Systems*, Available at: www.model.in.tum.de/um/courses/seminar/worm/WS0405/albag.pdf, Retrieved October 7, 2006.

[36]   D. Alessandri, *Attack-Class-Based Analysis of Intrusion Detection Systems*, *Ph.D. Thesis University of Newcastle upon Tyne, School of Computing Science*, Newcastle upon Tyne, UK, 2004.

[37]   J. Allen, A. Christie, W. Fithen, J. McHugh, J. Pickel and E. Stoner, *State of Practice of Intrusion Detection Technologies*, *Technical Report CMU/SEI-99-TR-028, CERT*, 1999.

[38]   D. Allesandri, C. Cachin, M. Dacier, O. Deak, K. Julisch, B. Randell, J. Riordan, A. Tscharner, A. Wespi and C. Wuest, *Towards a taxonomy of intrusion detection systems and attacks, Technical Report RZ 3366, IMB Research, Zurich Research Laboratory. MAFTIA project, report D3.*, 2001.

[39]   M. Almgren, E. L. Barse and E. Jonsson, *Consolidation and Evaluation of IDS Taxonomies, Eighth Nordic Workshop on Secure IT systems (NordSec2003)*, Gjøvik, Norway, October 15-17, 2003.

[40]   G. Alvarez and S. Petrovic, *Encoding a Taxonomy of Web Attacks with Different-Length Vectors, eprint arXiv:cs/0210026* Available at: http://arxiv.org/PS_cache/cs/pdf/0210/0210026.pdf, 10/2002

[41]   T. Anantvalee and J. Wu, *A Survey on Intrusion Detection in Mobile Ad Hoc Networks (Chapter 7)*, in Y. Xiao, X. Shen and D.-Z. Du, eds., Springer, 2006 pp. 170 - 196.

[42]   J. P. Anderson, *Computer Security Threat Monitoring and Surveillance, Technical Report. James P. Anderson Company* Fort Washington, Pennsylvania, April 1980.

[43]   A. D. Angeli, L. Coventry, G. I. Johnson and M. Coutts., *Usability and user authentication: Pictorial passwords vs. PIN., Contemporary Ergonomics, pages 253–258.*, Taylor & Francis, London, 2003.

[44]   S. Angle, R. Bhagtani and H. Chheda, *Biometrics: a Further Echelon of Security, The First UAE International Conference on Biological and Medical Physics*, 27 – 30 March, 2005.

[45]   F. Apap, A. Honig, S. Hershkop, E. Eskin and S. Stolfo, *Detecting malicious software by monitoring anomalous windows registry accesses, Technical report, CUCS Technical Report*, 2001.

[46]   B. Arkin, F. Hill, S. Marks, M. Schmid, T. J. Walls and G. McGraw, *How We Learned to Cheat in Online Poker: A Study in Software Security Developer.Com*, September 1999.

[47]   T. Aslam, I. Krsul and E. Spafford, *Use of A Taxonomy of Security Faults*, *19th National Information Systems Security Conference* Baltimore, MD, October 1996.

[48]   M. J. Atallah, E. D. Bryant and M. R. Stytz, *A Survey of Anti-Tamper Technologies*, *The Journal of Defense Software Engineering*, 2004, pp. 12-16.

[49]   A. Aussem, A. Mahul and R. Marie, *Queueing Network Modelling with Distributed Neural Networks for Service Quality Estimation in B-ISDN Networks*, Proceedings IEEE-INNS-ENNS International Joint Conference on Neural Networks (2000).

[50]   S. Axelsson, *Intrusion detection systems: a survey and taxonomy*, *Technical Report 99-15, Chalmers University*, 2000.

[51]   S. Axelsson, *Research in Intrusion Detection Systems: A Survey*, *Technical Report No. 98-17, Dept. of Computer Engineering, Chalmers University of Technology*, Göteborg, Sweden, 1999.

[52]   H. S. Baird and J. L. Bentley, *Implicit CAPTCHAs*, *In Proceedings of the SPIE/IS&T Conference on Document Recognition and Retrieval XII (DR&R2005)*, San Jose, CA, January, 2005.

[53]   H. S. Baird, M. A. Moll and S.-Y. W. :, *A Highly Legible CAPTCHA That Resists Segmentation Attacks*, *Human Interactive Proofs, Second International Workshop (HIP 2005)*, Bethlehem, PA, USA, May 19-20, 2005, pp. 27-41.

[54]   H. S. Baird, M. A. Moll and S.-Y. Wang, *ScatterType: a legible but hard-to-segment CAPTCHA*, *Proceedings of Eighth International Conference on Document Analysis and Recognition*, 29 Aug.-1 Sept. 2005, pp. 935- 939.

[55]   H. S. Baird and K. Popat, *Human Interactive Proofs and Document Image Analysis*, *Proceedings of the 5th International Workshop on Document Analysis Systems*, August 19-21, 2002 pp. 507-518.

[56]   H. S. Baird and T. Riopka, *ScatterType: a Reading CAPTCHA Resistant to Segmentation Attack*, Proc., *SPIE/IS&T Conf. on Document Recognition and Retrieval XII (DR&R2005)*, San Jose, CA, January 2005.

[57]   L. Ballard, D. Lopresti and F. Monrose, *Evaluating the Security of Handwriting Biometrics*, The 10th *International Workshop on Frontiers in Handwriting Recognition (IWFHR06)*, La Baule, France, October 2006, pp. 461-466.

[58]   L. Ballard, F. Monrose and D. P. Lopresti, *Biometric Authentication Revisited: Understanding the Impact of Wolves in Sheep's Clothing*, *Fifteenth USENIX Security Symposium*, Vancouver, BC, Canada, July-August 2006.

[59]   H. Banavar, *Security issues in Multi-player,Distributed Network Games*, Available at: http://ww2.cs.fsu.edu/~banavar/research/NSPaper.htm, Retrieved November 12, 2006.

[60]   M. Banikazemi, D. Poff and B. Abali, *Storage-based intrusion detection for storage area networks (SANs)*, Proceedings. 22nd IEEE / 13th NASA Goddard Conference on Mass Storage Systems and Technologies, 2005. , 11-14 April 2005, pp. 118- 127.

[61]   G. Bartolacci, M. Curtin, M. Katzenberg, N. Nwana, S.-H. Cha and C. C. Tappert, *Long-Text Keystroke Biometric Applications over the Internet*, *MLMTA* 2005, pp. 119-126.

[62]   B. G. Batchelor, *Pattern Recognition: Ideas in Practice*, Plenum Press (1978).

[63]   N. E. Baughman, M. Liberatore and B. N. Levine, *Cheat-Proof Playout for Centralized and Severless Online Games*, *IEEE/ACM Transactions on Networking*, December 2006.

[64]   E. Bekkering, M. Warkentin and K. Davis, *A Longitudinal Comparison of Four Password Procedures*, *Proceedings of the 2003 Hawaii International Conference on Business*, Honolulu, HI, June 2003.

[65]   S. D. Bella and C. Palmer, *Personal identifiers in musicians' finger movement dynamics*, Journal of Cognitive Neuroscience, 18 (2006).

[66]   C. BenAbdelkader, R. Cutler and L. Davis, *Person Identification using Automatic Height and Stride Estimation, IEEE International Conference on Pattern Recognition*, 2002.

[67]   J. Bentley and C. L. Mallows, *CAPTCHA challenge strings: problems and improvements, Document Recognition & Retrieval* 18-19 January 2006.

[68]   F. Bergadano, D. Gunetti and C. Picardi, *User authentication through keystroke dynamics, ACM Transactions on Information and System Security (TISSEC)*, November 2002 pp. 367-397.

[69]   S. Bhatkar, A. Chaturvedi and R. Sekar, *Dataflow Anomaly Detection, IEEE Symposium on Security and Privacy*, May 2006.

[70]   M. Bihina, J. Eloff and H. Venter, *Intrusion Detection Systems: Evolution and Future Direction, Honours Thesis. University of Pretoria, South Africa*, January 2004.

[71]   J.-C. Birget, D. Hong and N. Memon, *Robust Discretization, with an Application to Graphical Passwords*, Available at: citeseer.ist.psu.edu/birget03robust.html, Retrieved November 4, 2005.

[72]   M. Bishop, *Comparing Authentication Techniques*, Available at: citeseer.ist.psu.edu/bishop91comparing.html, Retrieved December 15, 2005.

[73]   M. Bishop, *Proactive Password Checking, 4th Workshop on Computer Security Incident Handling*, Available at: citeseer.ist.psu.edu/bishop92proactive.html, August 1992.

[74]   M. Bishop, *A taxonomy of unix system and network vulnerabilities, Technical Report CSE-9510, Department of Computer Science, University of California at Davis*, May 1995.

[75]   M. Bishop and D. Bailey, *A critical analysis of vulnerability taxonomies,*
        Tech. Rep.CSE-96-11, UC Davis Department of Computer Science,
        Available at http://www.cs.ucdavis.edu/research/tech-reports/1996/CSE-
        96-11.pdf, September 1996.

[76]   M. Bishop and D. Klein, *Improving System Security Through Proactive*
        Password Checking, Computers and Security 14 (3), May/June 1995, pp.
        233-249

[77]   A. Bivens, C. Palagiri, R. Smith, B. Szymanski and M. Embrechts,
        Network-Based Intrusion Detection Using Neural Networks, RPI (2001).

[78]   P. E. Black, *Traveling salesman from Dictionary of Algorithms and Data*
        Structures,   Available   at:
        http://www.nist.gov/dads/HTML/travelingSalesman.html   Retrieved
        October 22, 2005.

[79]   H. Blau, *The Human Nature of the Bot: a response to Philip Auslander,*
        PAJ: A Journal of Performance and Art, 24(1) (January 2002), pp. 22-24.

[80]   D. Blomqvist and J. Skantze, *Intrusion Detection: A study, Technical*
        Report Docs 95/62 Department of Computer Systems, Uppsala University,
        1995.

[81]   G. E. Blonder, *Graphical Passwords, United States Pattent 5559961,* 1996.

[82]   C. Blundo, P. D'Arco, A. D. Santis and C. Galdi, *Hyppocrates: A New*
        Proactive Password Checker, The Journal of Systems and Software, 2004,
        pp. 163-175.

[83]   R. Bolle, J. Connell, S. Pankanti, N. Ratha and A. Senior, *Guide to*
        Biometrics, Springer, 2003.

[84]   R. Brause, T. Langsdorf and M. Hepp, *Neural Data Mining for Credit Card*
        Fraud Detection, In Proceedings of the 11th IEEE International
        Conference on Tools with Artificial Intelligence, 1999, pp. 103--106.

[85]   A. Bromme, *A classification of biometric signatures*, International
        Conference on Multimedia and Expo (ICME '03) 6-9 July 2003, pp. 17-20.

[86]   A. Brömme and S. Al-Zubi, *Multifactor Biometric Sketch Authentication*,
        In A. Brömme and C. Busch, editors, Proceedings of the BIOSIG 2003,
        Darmstadt, Germany, 24. July 2003, pp. 81-90.

[87]   P. J. Brooke, R. F. Paige, J. A. Clark and S. Stepney, *Playing the game:
        cheating, loopholes, and virtual identity*, ACM SIGCAS Computers and
        Society, 34(2) (2004).

[88]   A. Brostoff, *Improving Password System Effectivness PhD Dissertation*,
        Department of Computer Science University College London, September
        30, 2004.

[89]   S. Brostoff and M. A. Sasse, *Are Passfaces More Usable Than Passwords?
        A Field Trial Investigation, Proceedings of CHI 2000, People and
        Computers XIV, pp. 405 - 424* Springer September 2000.

[90]   S. Brostoff, M. A. Sasse and D. Werich, *Transforming the `Weakest Link' --
        a Human/Computer Interaction Approach to Usable and Effective Security*,
        Technological Journal, July 2001, pp. 122-131.

[91]   C. C. Broun, X. Zhang, R. M. Mersereau and M. A. Clements, *Automatic
        Speechreading with Applications to Speaker Verification, Eurasip Journal
        on Applied Signal Processing, Special Issue on Joint Audio-Visual Speech
        Processing*, 2002.

[92]   B. J. Brown and K. Callis, *Computer Password Choice and Personality
        Traits Among College Students* Southeast Missouri State University
        Available   at: http://cstl-
        cla.semo.edu/callis/xResearch/PasswordsBettyBrown/PasswordsRevs5.30.0
        4.doc, Retrieved December 12, 2005.

[93]   I. Buhan and P. Hartel, *The state of the art in abuse of biometrics,
        Technical Report TR-CTIT-05-41 Centre for Telematics and Information
        Technology*, University of Twente, Enschede, 2005.

[94]   P. B.-d. Byl, *An Overview of Non-Player Characters in Games*, *Programming Believable Characters For Computer Games* Charles River Media, May 20, 2004.

[95]   M. Cahill, D. Lambert, J. Pinheiro and D. Sun, *Detecting fraud in the real world, Technical report, Bell Labs, Lucent Technologies*, 2000.

[96]   J. P. Campbell, *Speaker recognition: a tutorial*, Proceedings of the IEEE, 85(9) (Sep 1997), pp. 1437-1462.

[97]   J. Cannady, *Artificial Neural Networks for Misuse Detection*, Proceedings, National Information Systems Security Conference on Neural Networks (1998).

[98]   J. Cannady and J. Harrel, *A comparative Analysis of Current Intrusion Detection Technologies, Proceedings of Technology in Information Security Conference (TISC)*, 1996, pp. 212-218.

[99]   J. Cannady and J. Mahaffey, *The application of artificial intelligence to misuse detection*, Proceedings of the 1st Recent Advances in Intrusion Detection (RAID) Conference (1997).

[100] R. Cappelli, D. Maio, D. Maltoni, J. L. Wayman and A. K. Jain, *Performance Evaluation of Fingerprint Verification Systems*, IEEE Transactions on Pattern Analysis Machine Intelligence, 28 (January 2006), pp. 3-18.

[101] D. Carmel and S. Markovitch, *Learning Models of Opponent's Strategy in Game Playing, AAAI Fall Symposium on Intelligent Games: Planning and Learning*, The AAAI Press, Menlo Park, CA, 1993.

[102] G. A. Carpenter, S. Grossberg and N. Markuzon, *Fuzzy ARTMAP: A Neural Network Architecture for Incremental Supervised Learning of Analog Multidimensional Maps*, IEEE Transactions on Neural Networks, vol. 3 (1992).

[103] C. A. Carver, *An intrusion response taxonomy and its role in automatic intrusion response*, Proceedings of the 2000 IEEE Workshop on Information Assurance and Security, West Point, NY, USA, 2000.

[104] C. Chambers, W. C. Feng, W. C. Feng and D. Saha, *Mitigating Information Exposure to Cheaters in Real-Time Strategy Games*, Proceedings of NOSSDAV, June 2005.

[105] T.-Y. Chan, *Using a Text-to-Speech Synthesizer to Generate a Reverse Turing Test*, 15th IEEE International Conference on Tools with Artificial Intelligence (ICTAI'03), 2003, pp. 226.

[106] M. Chandrasekaran, R. Chinchani and S. Upadhyaya, *PHONEY: Mimicking User Response to Detect Phishing Attacks*, WOWMOM '06: Proceedings of the 2006 International Symposium on on World of Wireless, Mobile and Multimedia Networks, Washington, DC, USA, 2006, pp. 668--672.

[107] J. C. Checco, *Keystroke Dynamics & Corporate Security*, Available at: http://www.wsta.org/publications/articles/1003_article06.html, Retrieved October 2, 2005.

[108] K. Chellapilla, K. Larson, P. Simard and M. Czerwinski, *Designing Human Friendly Human Interaction Proofs (HIPs)*, Conference on Human factors In computing systems, ACM Press, 2005.

[109] K. Chellapilla, K. Larson, P. Y. Simard and M. Czerwinski, *Building Segmentation Based Human-Friendly Human Interaction Proofs (HIPs)*, in H. S. Baird and D. P. Lopresti, eds., *Human Interactive Proofs, Second International Workshop, HIP 2005, Bethlehem*, Springer, PA, USA, May 19-20, 2005, pp. 1-26.

[110] K. Chellapilla, K. Larson, P. Y. Simard and M. Czerwinski, *Computers beat Humans at Single Character Recognition in Reading based Human Interaction Proofs (HIPs)*, Second Conference on Email and Anti-Spam, California, USA, July 21-22, 2005.

[111] K. Chellapilla and P. Simard, *Using Machine Learning to Break Visual Human Interaction Proofs (HIPs), Advances in Neural Information Processing Systems 17, Neural Information Processing Systems (NIPS'2004)*, MIT Press.

[112] B. D. Chen and M. Maheswaran, *A cheat controlled protocol for centralized online multiplayer games, Proceedings of 3rd ACM SIGCOMM workshop on Network and system support for games*, Portland, Oregon, USA 2004, pp. 139 - 143

[113] K.-T. Chen, J.-W. Jiang, P. Huang, H.-H. Chu, C.-L. Lei and W.-C. Chen, *Identifying MMORPG Bots: A Traffic Analysis Approach, Proceedings of ACM SIGCHI ACE'06*, Los Angeles, USA, June 2006.

[114] W. Chen and M. Chen, *Internet Game Security*, Available at: http://islab.oregonstate.edu/koc/ece478/03Report/wtchen_mtchen.pdf.pdf, June 5th, 2002.

[115] M. Chew and H. S. Baird, *Baffletext: A human interactive proof, In Proceedings of SPIE-IS&T Electronic Imaging, Document Recognition and Retrieval X*, January 2003, pp. 305--316.

[116] M. Chew and J. D. Tygar, *Image Recognition Captchas, In proceedings of the 7th International Information Security Conference*, Springer, September 2004, pp. 268-279.

[117] R. Chinchani, A. Iyer, H. Ngo and S. Upadhyaya, *Towards a Theory of Insider Threat Assessment, IEEE International Conference on Dependable Systems and Networks (DSN 2005)*, Yokohama, Japan, June 2005.

[118] R. Chinchani, S. Upadhyaya and K. Kwiat, *Towards The Scalable Implementation Of A User Level Anomaly Detection System, IEEE MILCOM*, Anaheim, CA, October 2002.

[119] A. Chirichiello, *Automated Intrusion Detection*, Available at: www.dis.uniroma1.it/~dottorato/db/relazioni/relaz_chirichiello_1.pdf, Retrieved October 7, 2006.

[120] Z. Ciota, *Speaker verification for multimedia application, IEEE International Conference on Systems, Man and Cybernetics*, 10-13 Oct. 2004, pp. 2752- 2756.

[121] A. L. Coates, H. S. Baird and R. J. Fateman, *Pessimal print: A Reverse Turing Test, in Proc. of the Sixth Intl. Conf. on Document Analysis and Recognition*, Seattle, WA, September 2001, pp. 1154--1158.

[122] C. Collberg, C. Thomborson and D. Low, *A Taxonomy of Obfuscation Transformations, Technical Report 148, Department of Computer Science, University of Auckland*, July 1997.

[123] J. Colombi, D. Ruck, S. Rogers, M. Oxley and T. Anderson, *Cohort Selection and Word Grammer Effects for Speaker Recognition, IEEE International Conference on Acoustics, Speech, and Signal Processing*, Atlanta, GA, 1996, pp. 85-88.

[124] M. Consalvo, *Gaining Advantage: How videogame players define and negotiate cheating, Changing Views: Worlds in Play, second annual conference of the Digital Games Research Association*, Vancouver, British Columbia, June 2005.

[125] R. Coolen and H. A. M. Luiijf, *Intrusion Detection: Generics and State of the Art, NATO. Research & Technology Organisation. Technical Report. RTO-TR-049*, 2002.

[126] P. Crews, *Protochat: An Exploration of Natural Language Processing Proceedings of the 2006 CCEC Symposium*, Available at: http://symposium.ccec.unf.edu/cd/papers/Protochat_PCrews.pdf, 2006.

[127] M. Crompton, *Biometrics and privacy: The end of the world as we know it or the white knight of privacy?* , *1st Biometrics Institute Conference*, 2003.

[128] R. Cunningham and R. Lippmann, *Detecting Computer Attackers: recognizing patterns of malicious stealthy behavior*, MIT Lincoln Laboratory - Presentation to CERIAS (2000).

[129] R. Cunningham and R. Lippmann, *Improving Intrusion Detection performance using Keyword selection and Neural Networks*, MIT Lincoln University (1998).

[130] M. Curtin, C. C. Tappert, M. Villani, G. Ngo, J. Simone, H. S. Fort and S. Cha, *Keystroke Biometric Recognition on Long-Text Input: A Feasibility Study, Proc. Int. Workshop Sci Comp/Comp Stat (IWSCCS 2006)*, Hong Kong, June 2006.

[131] S. K. Dahel and Q. Xiao, *Accuracy performance analysis of multimodal biometrics, IEEE Information Assurance Workshop on Systems, Man and Cybernetics Society*, 18-20 June 2003, pp. 170- 173.

[132] M. Dailey and C. Namprempre, *A text graphics character CAPTCHA for password authentication, IEEE Region 10 Conference TENCON* 21-24 Nov. 2004, pp. 45- 48.

[133] V. Dao and V. Vemuri, *Profiling Users in the UNIX OS Environment, International ICSC Conference on Intelligent Systems and Applications*, University of Wollongong Australia, Dec. 11-15, 2000.

[134] D. Dasgupta and N. Attoh-Okine, *Immunity-based systems: a survey, IEEE International Conference on Systems, Man, and Cybernetics*, Orlando, FL, USA, 10/12/1997 - 10/15/1997, pp. 369-374.

[135] D. Davis, F. Monrose and M. K. Reiter, *On user choice in Graphical Password Schemes, In Proceedings of the 13th USENIX Security Symposium*, San Diego, August 2004.

[136] S. B. Davis, *Why cheating matters: Cheating, game security, and the future of global on-line game business, Proceedings of the 2001 Game Developers Conference*, 2001.

[137] H. Debar, M. Dacier and A. Wepsi, *A Revised Taxonomy for Intrusion-Detection Systems, IBM Research Report*, 1999.

[138] H. Debar, M. Dacier and A. Wespi, *Towards a Taxonomy of Intrusion-Detection Systems*, Computer Networks, 31 (1999), pp. 805-822.

[139] K. Delac and M. Grgic, *A Survey of Biometric Recognition Methods, 46th International Symposium Electronics in Marine, ELMAR-2004*, Zadar, Croatia, 16-18 June 2004, pp. 184-193.

[140] D. E. Denning, *An intrusion-detection model, IEEE Transactions on Software Engineering*, 1987, pp. 222-232.

[141] S. Deshpande, S. Chikkerur and V. Govindaraju, *Accent classification in speech, Fourth IEEE Workshop on Automatic Identification Advanced Technologies*, 17-18 Oct. 2005, pp. 139- 143.

[142] N. Desmarais, *Biometrics and Network Security, Available at:* http://www.acrlnec.org/sigs/itig/tc_nov_dec2000.htm, Retrieved October 2, 2005.

[143] R. Dhamija and A. Perrig, *Deja Vu: A User Study. Using Images for Authentication, Proceedings of the 9th USENIX Security Symposium*, Denver, Colorado August 2000.

[144] P. Doyle, *Virtual intelligence from artificial reality: Building stupid agents in smart environments, AAAI '99 Spring Symposium on Artificial Intelligence and Computer Games*, March 1999.

[145] R. O. Duda and P. E. Hart, *Pattern Classification and Scene Analysis*, Wiley (1973).

[146] J.-L. Dugelay, J.-C. Junqua, C. Kotropoulos, R. Kuhn, F. Perronnin and I. Pitas, *Recent advances in biometric person authentication, IEEE Int. Conf. on Acoustics Speech and Signal Processing (ICASSP), special session on biometrics*, Orlando, Florida, May 2002.

[147] M. M. Elissetche, *Social Science Dictionary, Available at:* http://www.elissetche.org/dico/P.htm, Retrieved October 6, 2005.

[148] C. Elkan, *Results of the KDD'99 Classifier Learning*, SIGKDD Explorations (2000).

[149] S. Enrique, A. Watt, S. C. Maddock and F. Policarpo, *Using Synthetic Vision for Autonomous Non-Player Characters*, Inteligencia Artificial, Revista Iberoamericana de Inteligencia Artificial, 21 (2003), pp. 19 - 25.

[150] H. Erdogan, A. Ercil, H. Ekenel, S. Bilgin, I. Eden, M. Kirisci and H. Abut, *Multi-modal person recognition for vehicular applications, N.C. Oza et al. (Eds.) MCS 2005, LNCS 3541*, Monterey CA, Jun. 2005, pp. 366 - 375.

[151] H. Erdogan, A. N. Ozyagci, T. Eskil, M. Rodoper, A. Ercil and H. Abut, *Experiments on decision fusion for driver recognition, Biennial on DSP for in-vehicle and mobile systems*, Sesimbra Portugal, Sep. 2005.

[152] L. Ertoz, M. Steinbach and V. Kumar, *Finding Clusters of Different Sizes, Shapes, and Densities in Noisy, High Dimensional Data*, Technical Report (2001).

[153] E. Erzin, Y. Yemez, A. M. Tekalp, A. Erçil, H. Erdogan and H. Abut, *Multimodal Person Recognition for Human-Vehicle Interaction*, *IEEE MultiMedia*, April 2006, pp. 18-31.

[154] S. Fagerland, S. Moon, K. Walls and C. Bretteville, *Norman Book on Computer Viruses*, Available at: http://download.norman.no/manuals/eng/BOOKON.PDF, Retrieved January 6, 2007.

[155] T. Fawcett and F. Provost, *Adaptive Fraud Detection, Data Mining and Knowledge Discovery*, Kluwer Academic Publishers, 1997 pp. 291-316.

[156] D. C. Feldmeier and P. R. Karn, *UNIX Password Security - Ten Years Later*, *CRYPTO*, Available at: citeseer.ist.psu.edu/188968.html, 1989, pp. 44-63.

[157] H. Feng, O. Kolesnikov, P. Fogla, W. Lee and W. Gong, *Anomaly Detection using Call Stack Information*, *Proceedings of the IEEE Security and Privacy*, Oakland, CA, USA, May 11-14, 2003.

[158] H. H. Feng, O. M. Kolesnikov, P. Fogla, W. Lee and W. Gong, *Anomaly detection using call stack information*, In *Proceedings of IEEE Symposium on Security and Privacy*, 2003, pp. 62-78.

[159] C. Y. Foo, *Redifining Grief Play*, *Other Players Conference*, Copenaghen, Denmark, 2004.

[160] C. Y. Foo and E. Koivisto, *Grief Player Motivations*, *Other Players Conference*, Copenaghen, Denmark, 2004.

[161] K. Fox, R. Henning and J. Reed, *A neural Network Approach Towards Intrusion Detection*, Proceedings of the 13th National Computer Security Conference (1990).

[162] J. Frank, *Artificial Intelligence and Intrusion Detection: Current and Future Directions*, *Proc.17th National Computer Security Conference, National Institute of Standards and Technology*, Washington,D.C, 1994, pp. 22-33.

[163] G. Frantzeskou, S. Gritzalis and S. MacDonell, *Source Code Authorship Analysis for Supporting the Cybercrime Investigation Process*, *1st International Conference on eBusiness and Telecommunication Networks - Security and Reliability in Information Systems and Networks Track*, Kluwer Academic Publishers, Setubal Portugal, August 2004, pp. 85-92.

[164] D. Freeman, *Creating Emotion in Games: The Craft and Art of Emotioneering*, ACM Computers in Entertainment, 2(3) (July 2004).

[165] R. French, *The turing test: The first fifty years*, 4(3) (2000), pp. 115-121.

[166] Y. Fu and M. Shih, *A Framework for Personal Web Usage Mining*, *International Conference on Internet Computing (IC'2002)*, Las Vegas, NV, June, 2002, pp. 595-600.

[167] H. Gamboa and V.-. A. Fred ., 2004., *A Behavioral Biometric System Based on Human Computer Interaction*, *In Proceedings of SPIE*, 2004.

[168] H. Gamboa and A. Fred, *An identity authentication system based on human computer interaction behaviour*, *Proc. of the 3rd Intl. Workshop on Pattern Recognition in Information Systems*, ICEIS PRESS, 2003, pp. 46 -55.

[169] R. Ganesan and C. Davies, *A new attack on random pronouncable password generators*, *In 17th NIST-NCSC National Computer Security Conference*, 1994, pp. 184-- 197.

[170] A. Garg, R. Rahalkar, S. Upadhyaya and K. Kwiat, *Profiling Users in GUI Based Systems for Masquerade Detection*, *The 7th IEEE Information Assurance Workshop (IAWorkshop 2006)* West Point, New York, USA, June 21-23, 2006

[171] A. K. Ghosh, A. Schwatzbard and M. Shatz, *Learning Program Behavior Profiles for Intrusion Detection, in Proceedings 1 st USENIX Workshop on Intrusion Detection and Network Monitoring*, Santa Clara, California, April 1999.

[172] J. Giffin, S. Jha and B. Miller, *Efficient context-sensitive intrusion detection*, *In 11th Annual Network and Distributed Systems Security Symposium (NDSS)*, San Diego, California, February 2004.

[173] L. Girardin and D. Brodbeck, *A Visual Approach for Monitoring Logs*, 12th System Administration Conference (LISA '98) (1998), pp. 299-308.

[174] J. Goecks and J. Shavlik, *Learning Users' Interests by Unobtrusively Observing Their Normal Behavior*, *Proceedings of the 2000 International Conference on Intelligent User Interfaces*, New Orleans, LA, 2000, pp. 129-132.

[175] T. Goldring, *User Profiling for Intrusion Detection in Windows NT*, Computing Science and Statistics, 35 (2003).

[176] P. Golle and N. Ducheneaut, *Preventing bots from playing online games*, ACM Computers in Entertainment, 3(3) (July 2005).

[177] P. Gollé and N. Ducheneaut, *Keeping bots out of online games, ACM SIGCHI International Conference on Advances in Computer Entertainment Technology*, Valencia; Spain, 2005 June 15-17.

[178] A. Gray, P. Sallis and S. MacDonell, *Software Forensics: Extending Authorship Analysis Techniques to Computer Programs, In Proc. 3rd Biannual Conf. Int. Assoc. of Forensic Linguists (IAFL'97)*, 1997.

[179] J. L. Griffin, A. G. Pennington, J. S. Bucy, D. Choundappan, N. Muralidharan and G. R. Ganger, *On the Feasibility of Intrusion Detection Inside Workstation Disks, Technical Report CMU-PDL-03-106, Carnegie Mellon University*, 2003.

[180] H. Grosser, H. Britos and R. García-Martínez, *Detecting Fraud in Mobile Telephony Using Neural Networks, Lecture Notes in Artificial Intelligence*, Springer-Verlag, 2005, pp. 613-615.

[181] D. Gunetti, C. Picardi and G. Ruffo, *Keystroke Analysis of Different Languages: a Case Study, Proc. of the Sixth Symposium on Intelligent Data Analysis (IDA 2005)*, Springer-Verlag, Madrid, Spain, 2005, pp. 133-144.

[182] G. Gupta, C. Mazumdar and M. S. Rao, *Digital Forensic Analysis of E-mails: A trusted E-mail Protocol*, International Journal of Digital Evidence, 2 (2004).

[183] R. V. Hall, *CAPTCHA as a Web Security Control*, Available at: www.richhall.com/isc4350/captcha_20051217.htm, Retrieved October 26, 2006.

[184] H. v. Halteren, *Linguistic profiling for author recognition and verification, In Proceedings of ACL-2004*, 2004.

[185] F. M. Ham, *Principles of Neurocomputing for Science and Engineering*, McGraw Hill (1991).

[186] S. Hansman and R. Hunt, *A taxonomy of network and computer attacks*, Computers & Security, 24 (2005), pp. 31-43.

[187] S. Hart, *Comments of Privacilla.org on Formulating and Conducting a Study of Biometrics and Similar Technologies to Combat Identity Theft*, Available   at: *http://www.privacilla.org/releases/FACT_Act_Biometric_Study.html*, Retrieved October 2, 2005.

[188] J. A. Hartigan, *Clustering Algorithms*, John Wiley and Sons (1975).

[189] E. Hayes, *Playing it Safe: Avoiding Online Gaming Risks*, Available at: http://www.us-cert.gov/reading_room/gaming.pdf, Retrieved October 30, 2006.

[190] N. J. Henderson, N. M. White, R. N. J. Veldhuis, P. H. Hartel and C. H. Slump, *Sensing pressure for authentication, 3rd IEEE Benelux Signal Processing Symp. (SPS)*, Leuven, Belgium, 2002, pp. 241-244.

[191] N. Y. Henderson, T. V. Papakostas, N. M. White and P. H. Hartel, *Polymer Thick-Film Sensors: Possibilities for Smartcard Biometrics Proceedings of Sensors and their applications XI*, 2001, pp. 83-88.

[192] B. Herbst and *H. Coetzer, On an offline signature verification system, Proceedings of the 9th Annual South African Workshop on Pattern Recognition*, 1998, pp. 39-43.

[193] H. J. v. d. Herik, H. H. L. M. Donkers and P. H. M. Spronck, *Opponent Modelling and Commercial Games, IEEE 2005 Symposium on Computational Intelligence and Games CIG05*, Colchester, UK, 2005, pp. 15-25.

[194] M. Hertzum, *Remembering Multiple Passwords by Way of Minimal-Feedback Hints: Replication and Further Analysis, Proceedings of the Fourth Danish Human-Computer Interaction Research Symposium*, Aalborg University, Aalborg, DK, November 16, 2004, pp. 21-24.

[195] S. Hettich and S. D. Bay, *The UCI KDD Archive*, University of California, Department of Information and Computer Science (1999).

[196] C. Hilas and J. Sahalos, *User Profiling for Fraud Detection in Telecommunication Networks 5th International Conference on Technology and Automation (ICTA 2005)*, Thessaloniki, Greece 15-16 October 2005 pp. 382-387

[197] B. Hoanca and K. Mock, *Screen oriented technique for reducing the incidence of shoulder surfing, The 2005 Internation Conference on Security and Management*, Las Vegas, June 20-23, 2005.

[198] S. A. Hofmeyr, S. Forrest and A. Somayaji, *Intrusion detection using sequences of system calls, Journal of Computer Security*, 1998, pp. 151--180.

[199] J. D. Howard, *An analysis of security incidents on the Internet 1989-1995, Department of Engineering and Public Policy*, Carnegie Mellon University, 1998.

[200] A. Humm, J. Hennebert and R. Ingold, *Scenario and Survey of Combined Handwriting and Speech Modalities for User Authentication, 6th International Conference on Recent Advances in Soft Computing (RASC'06)*, Canterbury (UK), July 10-12 2006, pp. 496 - 501.

[201] K. Igarashi, C. Miyajima, K. Itou, K. Takeda, F. Itakura and H. Abut, *Biometric identification using driving behavioral signals, Proc. 2004 IEEE International Conference on Multimedia and Expo*, 2004, pp. 65-68.

[202] K. Ilgun, R. A. Kemmerer and P. A. Porras, *State transition analysis: A rule-based intrusion detection approach, Software Engineering*, 1995, pp. 181-199.

[203] J. Ilonen, *Keystroke dynamics*, Available at: www.it.lut.fi/kurssit/03-04/010970000/seminars/Ilonen.pdf, Retrieved July 12, 2006.

[204] A. Ito, X. Wang, M. Suzuki and S. Makino, *Smile and Laughter Recognition using Speech Processing and Face Recognition from Conversation Video, Proceedings of the 2005 International Conference on Cyberworlds*, 2005, pp. 437-444

[205] K. Jackson, *Intrusion Detection System Product Survey Technical Report: LA-UR-99-3883*, Los Alamos National Laboratory, Los Alamos, New Mexico, USA, 1999.

[206] B. A. Jacob and S. D. Levitt, *To catch a cheat*, *Education next*, Availablet at: www.educationnext.org, 2004.

[207] A. Jain, F. Griess and S. Connell, *On-line signature verification*, *Pattern Recognition*, 2002, pp. 2963--2972.

[208] A. K. Jain, R. Bolle and S. Pankanti, *BIOMETRICS: Personal Identification in Networked Society*, Kluwer Academic Publishers, 1999.

[209] A. K. Jain, S. C. Dass and K. Nandakumar, *Can soft biometric traits assist user recognition?*, *Proceedings of SPIE Defense and Security Symposium*, Orlando, FL, April 2004.

[210] A. K. Jain, S. C. Dass and K. Nandakumar, *Soft Biometric Traits for Personal Recognition Systems*, *Proc. International Conference on Biometric Authentication (ICBA)*, Hong Kong, July 2004, pp. 731-738.

[211] A. K. Jain, S. Pankanti, S. Prabhakar, L. Hong and A. Ross, *Biometrics: A Grand Challenge*, *Proceedings of the International Conference on Pattern Recognition*, Cambridge, UK, August 2004.

[212] A. K. Jain, A. Ross and S. Prabhakar, *An introduction to biometric recognition*, *IEEE Trans. Circuits Syst. Video Technol*, 2004, pp. 4-20.

[213] K. Jain, K. Nandakumar and A. Ross, *Score normalization in multimodal biometric systems*, *Pattern Recognition*, 2005, pp. 2270--2285.

[214] M. G. Janowski and A. H. Sung, *Intrusion Detection Using Neural Networks and Support Vector Machines*, *Proceedings of IEEE IJCNN*, 2002, pp. 1702-1707.

[215] A. R. Jansen, D. L. Dowe and G. E., *Farr Inductive Inference of Chess Player Strategy*, *Proceedings of the 6th Pacific Rim International Conference on Artificial Intelligence (PRICAI'2000)*, 2000, pp. 61-71.

[216] W. Jansen, S. Gavrila, V. Korolev, R. Ayers and R. Swanstrom, *Picture Password: A Visual Login Technique for Mobile Devices* Available at: http://csrc.nist.gov/publications/nistir/nistir-7030.pdf, Retrieved October 24, 2005.

[217] N. D. Jayaram and P. L. R. Morse, *Network security-a taxonomic view*, *European Conference on Security and Detection, ECOS 97*, London, UK, 28-30 April 1997, pp. 124-127.

[218] I. Jermyn, A. Mayer, F. Monrose, M. K. Reiter and A. D. Rubin, *The Design and Analysis of Graphical Passwords Proceedings of the 8th USENIX Security Symposium*, Washington, D.C., August 23-36, 1999.

[219] E. Jervis, M. Kennedy, N. Kepler and J. Kim, *Trends in Biometrics and User Acceptance*, Available at: http://www.simson.net/ref/2005/csci_e-170/p1/future.pdf, Retrieved August 3, 2006.

[220] A. B. Jianxin (Jeff) Yan, Ross Anderson and Alasdair Grant, *The Memorability and Security of Passwords -- Some Empirical Results.* , *Technical Report No. 500*, Computer Laboratory, University of Cambridge, Available at: http://www.ftp.cl.cam.ac.uk/ftp/users/rja14/tr500.pdf, 2000.

[221] A. K. Jones and R. S. Sielken, *Computer System Intrusion Detection: A Survey*, *Computer Science Technical Report* University of Virginia, 2000.

[222] P. Jourlin, J. Luettin, D. Genoud and H. Wassner, *Acoustic-labial speaker verification*, *Pattern Recognition Letters*, 1997, pp. 853--858.

[223] T. W. S. Journal, *Watch on the Thames*, Available at: http://online.wsj.com/public/article/SB112077340647880052-cKyZgAb0T3asU4UDFVNPWrOAqCY_20060708.html, Retrieved October 4, 2005.

[224] P. Juola and J. Sofko, *Proving and Improving Authorship Attribution*, *Proceedings of CaSTA-04 The Face of Text*, 2004.

[225] P. Kabiri and A. A. Ghorbani, *Research on Intrusion Detection and Response: A Survey*, International Journal of Network Security, September 2005 pp. 84-102.

[226] P. Kabus, W. Terpstra, M. Cilia and A. Buchmann, *Addressing Cheating in Distributed Massively Multiplayer Online Games*, In Proc. of Intl Workshop on NetGames, October 2005.

[227] J. Kaiser and M. Reichenbach, *Evaluating Security Tools towards Usable Security: A Usability Taxonomy for the Evaluation of Security Tools Based on a Categorization of User Errors*, The IFIP 17th World Computer Congress - TC13 Stream on Usability: Gaining a Competitive Edge 2002 pp. 247 - 256

[228] A. Kale, A. Sundaresan, A. N. Rajagopalan, N. Cuntoor, A. RoyChowdhury, V.Kruger and R. Chellappa, *Identification of humans using gait*, IEEE Transactions on Image Processing, July 2004.

[229] S. Kalyanaraman, *Biometric Authentication Systems A Report*, Available at: http://netlab.cs.iitm.ernet.in/cs650/2006/TermPapers/sriramk.pdf, Retrieved July 26, 2006.

[230] M. Karresand, *A Proposed Taxonomy for IT Weapons*, 7th Nordic Workshop on Secure IT Systems, SimoneFisher-Hübner and Erland Jonsson, Eds, Karlstad, Sweden, November 2002, pp. 244-260.

[231] M. Karresand, *Separating Trojan horses, viruses, and worms - a proposed taxonomy of software weapons*, IEEE Systems, Man and Cybernetics Society Information Assurance Workshop, 18-20 June 2003, pp. 127- 134.

[232] J. A. Kauffman, A. M. Bazen, S. H. Gerez and R. N. J. Veldhuis, *Grip-pattern recognition for smart guns*, 14th Annual Workshop on Circuits, Systems and Signal Processing (ProRISC), Veldhoven, The Netherlands, 2003, pp. 379-384.

[233] K. Kaufman, G. Cervone and R. S. Michalski, *An Application of Symbolic Learning to Intrusion Detection: Preliminary Results From the LUS*

Methodology, Reports of the Machine Learning and Inference Laboratory, MLI 03-2, George Mason University, Fairfax, VA, June, 2003.

[234] G. Kayacik, N. Zincir-Heywood and M. Heywood, *On the Capability of an SOM based Intrusion Detection System*, IEEE 0-7803-7898-9 (2003).

[235] R. A. Kemmerer and G. Vigna, *Intrusion Detection: A Brief History and Overview*, IEEE Security and Privacy, 35(4) (Apr. 2002), pp. 27-30.

[236] G. C. Kessler, *Passwords - Strengths and weaknesses, Internet and Internetworking Security*, Auerbach, Available at: http://www.garykessler.net/library/password.html, January 1996.

[237] V. Kher and Y. Kim, *Securing distributed storage: challenges, techniques, and systems ACM workshop on Storage security and survivability* Fairfax, VA, USA 2005 pp. 9 - 25

[238] K. S. Killourhy, R. A. Maxion and K. M. C. Tan, *A defense-centric taxonomy based on attack manifestations, International Conference on Dependable Systems and Networks*, Pittsburgh, PA, USA;, 28 June-1 July 2004, pp. 102- 111.

[239] Y. Kim, J.-Y. Jo and K. Suh, *Baseline Profile Stability for Network Anomaly Detection, IEEE ITNG 2006, Internet and Wireless Network Security track*, Las Vegas, NV, April 2006.

[240] K. K. Kimppa and A. K. Bissett, *The Ethical Significance of Cheating in Online Computer Games*, International Review of Information Ethics, 4 (December 2005).

[241] D. V. Klein, *Foiling the cracker : A survey of and improvements to password security, USENIX Conference Proceedings*, 1990.

[242] C. Kline and B. Blumberg, *The Art and Science of Synthetic Character Design, Symposium on AI and Creativity in Entertainment and Visual Art*, Edinburgh, Scotland, 1999.

[243] C. Ko, G. Fink and K. Levitt, *Automated detection of vulnerabilities in privileged programs by execution monitoring*, In Proceedings of the 10th Annual Computer Security Applications Conference, December 1994, pp. 134-- 144.

[244] G. Kochanski, D. Lopresti and C. Shih, *A reverse turing test using speech*, Proceedings of the International Conferences on Spoken Language Processing, Denver, Colorado, 2002, pp. 1357--1360.

[245] M. Koppel and J. Schler, *Authorship Verification as a One-Class Classification Problem*, in Proceedings of 21st International Conference on Machine Learning, Banff, Canada, July 2004, pp. 489-495.

[246] M. Koppel, J. Schler and D. Mughaz, *Text Categorization for Authorship Verification*, Eighth International Symposium on Artificial Intelligence and Mathematics, Fort Lauderdale, Florida, Januray 2004.

[247] I. Koychev and I. Schwab, *Adaptation to Drifting User's Interests*, In Proceedings of ECML2000 Workshop: Machine Learning in New Information Age, Barcelona, Spain, 2000.

[248] I. Krsul and *Computer vulnerability analysis thesis proposal*, Technical Report CSD-TR-97-026, Computer Science Department, Purdue University, 1997.

[249] C. Krugel and T. Toth, *A Survey on Intrusion Detection Systems*, Technical reportTUV- 1841-00-11 , Technical University of Vienna , Information Systems institute, December 2000.

[250] J. Kuecklich, *Other Playings - Cheating in Computer Games* Available at: http://itu.dk/op/papers/kuecklich.pdf, December 2004.

[251] N. Kuge, T. Yamamura and O. Shimoyama, *A driver behavior recognition method based on driver model framework. *, Society of Automotive Engineers Publication, 1998.

[252] S. Kumar, *Classification and Detection of Computer Intrusions*, Ph.D. Dissertation Purdue University, August 1995.

[253] A. Kuo, *A (very) brief history of cheating*, Available at: http://shl.stanford.edu/Game_archive/StudentPapers/BySubject/A-I/C/Cheating/Kuo_Andy.pdf, Retrieved: November 12, 2006.

[254] H. Kvarnström, *A survey of commercial tools for intrusion detection, Technical report No99-8, Chalmers University of Technology, Depart. of Computer Engineering*, Sweden, 1999.

[255] J. Laird and J. Duchi, *Creating human-like synthetic characters with multiple skill levels: A case study using the soar quakebot, Proceedings of the 2000 AAAI Fall Symposium: Simulating Human Agents. M. Freed (editor).*

[256] J. E. Laird, *Using Computer Games to Develop Advanced AI*, Computer, 34(7) (2001), pp. 70-75.

[257] L.-c. Lam, W. Li and T.-c. Chiueh, *Accurate and Automated System Call Policy-Based Intrusion Prevention, in Proceedings of 2006 International Conference on Dependable Systems and Networks (DSN 2006)*, June 2006

[258] C. E. Landwehr, A. R. Bull, J. P. McDermott and W. Choi, *A Taxonomy of Computer Program Security Flaws with Examples, NRL Report 9591, Naval Research Laboratory*, November 1993.

[259] T. Lane and C. E. Brodley, *An Application of Machine Learning to Anomaly Detection, 20th Annual National Information Systems Security Conference*, 1997, pp. 366-380.

[260] T. Lane and C. E. Brodley, *Detecting the Abnormal: Machine Learning in Computer Security, Department of Electrical and Computer Engineering, Purdue University Technical Report ECE-97-1*, West Lafayette, January 1997.

[261] A. Lazarevic, L. Ertoz, V. Kumar, A. Ozgur and J. Srivastava, *A comparative study of anomaly detection schemes in network intrusion detection, In Proceedings of the Third SIAM International Conference on Data Mining*, 2003.

[262]   A. Lazarevic, V. Kumar and J. Srivastava, *Intrusion Detection-A Survey, Managing Cyber Threats-Issues, Approaches, and Challenges,*, Springer, 2005, pp. 19-80.

[263]   A. Ledezma, R. Aler, A. Sanchis and D. Borrajo, *Predicting Opponent Actions by Observation, RoboCup*, Lisbon, Portugal, June, 2004.

[264]   K. Lee and H. Park, *A New Similarity Measure Based on Intraclass Statistics for Biometric Systems, ETRI Journal*, Oct. 2003, pp. 401-406.

[265]   W. Lee, S. Stolfo and K. Mok, *Mining in a Data-Flow Environment: Eperience in Network Intrusion Detection*, In Proceedings of the 5th ACM SIGKDD (1999).

[266]   W. Lee, S. J. Stolfo and K. W. Mok, *A Data Mining Framework for Building Intrusion Detection Models, IEEE Symposium on Security and Privacy*, Okland, CA, 1999.

[267]   W. Lee, S. J. Stolfo and K. W. Mok, *A Data Mining Framework for Building Intrusion Detection Models*, IEEE Symposium on Security and Privacy (1999).

[268]   Y. Lee, *Classifiers: Adaptive Modules in Pattern Recognition Systems*, Cambridge, MA: MIT (1989).

[269]   H. Lei, S. Palla and V. Govindaraju, *ER2: An Intuitive Similarity Measure for On-Line Signature Verification, IWFHR '04: Proceedings of the Ninth International Workshop on Frontiers in Handwriting Recognition (IWFHR'04)*, IEEE Computer Society, 2004, pp. 191--195.

[270]   I. Levin, *KDD-99 Classifier Learning Contest LLSoft's Results Overview*, SIGKDD Explorations, vol. 1 (2000).

[271]   K. Li, S. Ding, D. McCreary and S. Webb, *Analysis of State Exposure Control to Prevent Cheating in Online Games, ACM Nossdav* Kinsale, County Cork, Ireland, 2004.

[272] S. Li and H.-Y. Shum, *Secure Human-Computer Identification against Peeping Attacks*, Available at: citeseer.ist.psu.edu/li03secure.html, Retrieved November 4, 2005.

[273] Y. Li, N. Wu, S. Jajodia and X. S. Wang, *Enhancing Profiles for Anomaly Detection Using Time Granularities, Journal of Computer Security*, 2002, pp. 137-157.

[274] T. P. Liang and H.-J. Lai, *Discovering User Interests from Web Browsing Behavior, Proceedings of the Hawaii International Conference on Systems Sciences*, Hawaii, USA, 2002

[275] W.-H. Liao, *A Captcha Mechanism By Exchange Image Blocks, 18th International Conference on Pattern Recognition (ICPR'06)*, 2006, pp. 1179-1183.

[276] W.-H. Liao and C.-C. Chang, *Embedding information within dynamic visual patterns, IEEE International Conference on Multimedia and Expo ICME '04.* , 27-30 June 2004, pp. 895- 898.

[277] J. Liddell, K. Renaud and A. D. Angeli, *Using a Combination of Sound and Images to Authenticate Web Users, 17th Annual Human Computer Interaction Conference. Designing for Society*, Bath, England, 8-12 Sept, 2003.

[278] X. Lin and S. Simske, *Phoneme-less hierarchical accent classification, Conference Record of the Thirty-Eighth Asilomar Conference on Signals, Systems and Computers* 7-10 Nov. 2004, pp. 1801- 1804.

[279] U. Lindqvist and E. Jonsson, *How to Systematically Classify Computer Security Intrusions, Proc. Symp. Security and Privacy*, 1997.

[280] A. Liu and D. Salvucci, *Modeling and Prediction of Human Driver Behavior, Proc. of the 9th HCI International Conference*, New Orleans, LA, Aug. 5-10, 2001, pp. 1479-1483.

[281] D. Liu and F. Huebner, *Application Profiling of IP Traffic*, *27th Annual IEEE Conference on Local Computer Networks*, Nov. 6-8, 2002, pp. 220-229.

[282] Z. Liu and S. M. Bridges, *Dynamic learning of automata from the call stack log for anomaly detection*, *International Conference on Information Technology: Coding and Computing (ITCC 2005)*, 4-6 April 2005, pp. 774-779.

[283] D. Lopresti, *Leveraging the CAPTCHA problem*, *Proceedings of the Second HIP Conference*, 2005.

[284] J. Luettin, N. A. Thacker and S. W. Beet, *Speaker identification by lipreading*, *Proceedings of the 4th International Conference on Spoken Language Processing (ICSLP'96)*, 1996.

[285] E. Lundin and E. Jonsson, *Survey of intrusion detection research*, *Chalmers University, Technical. Report*, February 2002.

[286] T. Lunt, *Detecting Intruders in Computer Systems*, *In Proceedings of the 1993 Conference on Auditing and Computer Technology*, 1993.

[287] T. F. Lunt, *Automated Audit Trail Analysis and Intrusion Detection: A Survey*, *Proceedings of the 11th National Computer Security Conference*, Baltimore, MD, October 1998.

[288] Y. Lyhyaoui, A. Lyhyaoui and S. Natkin, *Online Games: Categorization of Attacks*, *The International Conference on Computer as a Tool (EUROCON 2005)*, 21-24 Nov. 2005, pp. 1340- 1343.

[289] S. Lyu, D. Rockmore and H. Farid, *A Digital Technique for Art Authentication*, *Proceedings of the National Academy of Sciences*, 2004 pp. 17006-17010.

[290] M. Mahoney, *Computer Security: A Survey of Attacks and Defenses*, Available at: http://www.cs.fit.edu/~mmahoney/ids.html, September 11, 2000.

[291] J.-F.   Mainguet,   *Biometrics*,   Available   at:
http://perso.orange.fr/fingerchip/biometrics/biometrics.htm, Retrieved July
28, 2006.

[292] C. Marceau, *Characterizing the Behavior of a Program Using Multiple-
Length N-grams, Proceedings of the New Security Paradigms Workshop
2000*, Cork, Ireland, Sept. 19-21, 2000.

[293] J. Marin, D. Ragsdale and J. Surdu, *A hybrid approach to the profile
creation and intrusion detection, DARPA Information Survivability
Conference and Exposition (DISCEX II'01)*, 2001.

[294] J. S. D. Mason, J. Brand, R. Auckenthaler, F. Deravi and C. Chibelushi, *Lip
Signatures for Automatic Person Recognition, In IEEE Workshop, MMSP*,
1999, pp. 457--462.

[295] S. Mathew, C. Shah and S. Upadhyaya, *An Alert Fusion Framework for
Situation Awareness of Multistage Coordinated Attacks, IEEE International
Workshop on Information Assurance*, Washington DC, March 2005.

[296] R. A. Maxion and T. N. Townsend, *Masquerade Detection Using
Truncated Command Lines, International Conference od Dependable
Systems and Networks*, Washington, DC, June 23-26, 2002.

[297] R. A. Maxion and T. N. Townsend, *Masquerade detection using truncated
command lines, In International conference on dependable systems and
networks(DNS-02)*, IEEE Computer Society Press, 2002.

[298] M. May, *Inaccessibility of CAPTCHA. Alternatives to Visual Turing Tests
on the Web, W3C Working Group Note*, Availablet at:
www.w3.org/TR/turingtest/ November 2005.

[299] N. McAuliffe, D. Wolcott, L. Schaefer, N. Kelem, B. Hubbard and T.
Haley, *Is your computer being misused? A survey of current
intrusiondetection system technology, Proceedings of the Sixth Annual
Computer Security Applications Conference*, Tucson, AZ, USA, 3-7 Dec
1990, pp. 260-272.

[300] D. L. McDonald, R. J. Atkinson and C. Metz, *One Time Passwords In Everything (OPIE): Experiences with Building and Using Stronger Authentication Proceedings of teh Fifth USENIX UNIX Security Symposium*, Sal Lake City, Utah, June 1995.

[301] C. Meadows, *An outline of a taxonomy of computer security research and development Proceedings on the 1992-1993 workshop on New security paradigms*, Little Compton, Rhode Island, United States 1993 pp. 33 - 35

[302] P. Mell, V. Hu, R. Lipmann, J. Haines and M. Zissman, *An overview of issues in testing intrusion detection systems, Technical Report NIST IR 7007, National Institute of Standard and Technology*, July 2003.

[303] C. C. Michael, *Finding the vocabulary of program behavior data for anomaly detection, DARPA Information Survivability Conference and Exposition, 2003*, 22-24 April 2003, pp. 152- 163.

[304] C. C. Michael and A. Ghosh, *Using finite automata to mine execution data for intrusion detection: A preliminary report, In Proceedings of the Third International Workshop in Recent Advances in Intrusion Detection*, Toulouse, France, October 2000.

[305] J. Mirkovic, P. Reiher and *A taxonomy of DDoS attack and DDoS defense mechanisms* ACM SIGCOMM Computer Communication Review 34(2) (2004), pp. 39 - 53.

[306] D. Misra and K. Gaj, *Face Recognition CAPTCHAs, International Conference on Telecommunications, Internet and Web Applications and Services (AICT-ICIW '06)*, 19-25 Feb. 2006, pp. 122.

[307] L. Mok, W. H. Lau, S. H. Leung, S. L. Wang and H. Yan, *Person authentication using ASM based lip shape and intensity information International Conference on Image Processing*, 24-27 Oct. 2004, pp. 561- 564.

[308] J. Mölsä, *A Taxonomy of Criteria for Evaluating Defence Mechanisms against Flooding DoS Attacks, Proceedings of the 1st European*

Conference on Computer Network Defence, Pontypridd, Wales, UK, December, 2005.

[309] F. Monrose, M. K. Reiter and S. Wetzel, *Password Hardening based on Keystroke Dynamics, International Journal of Information Security, 1(1):69--83*, 2001.

[310] F. Monrose and A. D. Rubin, *Keystroke Dynamics as a Biometric for Authentication, Future Generation Computing Systems (FGCS) Journal: Security on the Web (special issue)*, March 2000.

[311] K. Mørch, *Cheating in online games- threats and solutions, Publication No: DART/01/03. Norwegian Computing Center/Applied Research and Development*, January 2003.

[312] G. Mori and J. Malik, *Recognizing objects in adversarial clutter: breaking a visual CAPTCHA, Proceedings of IEEE Computer Society Conference on Computer Vision and Pattern Recognition* 18-20 June 2003, pp. I-134- I-141.

[313] R. Morris and K. Thompson, *Password Security: a Case History, CACM,* 1979, pp. 594--597.

[314] G. Moy, N. Jones, C. Harkless and R. Potter, *Distortion estimation techniques in solving visual CAPTCHAs, Proceedings of the 2004 IEEE Computer Society Conference on Computer Vision and Pattern Recognition (CVPR 2004)* 27 June-2 July 2004, pp. II-23- II-28.

[315] C. Moyer, *How Intelligent is a Game Bot, Anyway?, Available at: http://www.tcnj.edu/~games/AIGames/papers/Moyer.html,* Retrieved January 9, 2007.

[316] N. Muralidharan and S. Wunnava, *Signature Verification: A Popular Biometric technology Second LACCEI International Latin American and Caribbean Conference for Engineering and Technology (LACCEI'2004)* Miami, Florida, USA, 2-4 June 2004.

[317] D. Nali and J. Thorpe., *Analyzing User Choice in Graphical Passwords.*, *Tech. Report TR-04-01, School of Computer Science Carleton University*, Canada, 2004.

[318] V. S. Nalwa, *Automatic On-line Signature Verification, Proceedings of the IEEE*, Feb.1997, pp. 215-239.

[319] B. M. Namee, S. Dobbyn, P. Cunningham and C. O'Sullivan, *Simulating Virtual Humans Across Diverse Situations, Springer lecture notes in AI (Proceedings Intelligent Virtual Agents)*, 2003, pp. 159 - 163.

[320] M. Naor, *Verification of a human in the loop or identification via the turing test*, Available at: http://www.wisdom.weizmann.ac.il/~naor/PAPERS/human_abs.html, 1996. Retrieved October 7, 2006.

[321] A. Narayanan and V. Shmatikov, *Fast dictionary attacks on passwords using time-space tradeoff Conference on Computer and Communications Security archive Proceedings of the 12th ACM conference on Computer and communications security* Alexandria, VA, USA, 2005, pp. 364 - 372.

[322] N. Nguyen, P. Reiher and G. H. Kuenning, *Detecting insider threats by monitoring system call activity, IEEE Systems, Man and Cybernetics Society Information Assurance Workshop*, 18-20 June 2003, pp. 45- 52.

[323] S. Nielson, S. Crosby and D. Wallach, *A Taxonomy of Rational Attacks, In Proc. of IPTPS*, Ithaca, NY, February 2005.

[324] M. S. Nixon and J. N. Carter, *On Gait as a Biometric: Progress and Prospects In Proceedings of Proc. EUSIPCO 2004*, Vienna.

[325] D. Novikov, R. V. Yampolskiy and L. Reznik, *Anomaly Detection Based Intrusion Detection, Third International Conference on Information Technology: New Generations (ITNG 2006)*, Las Vegas, Nevada, USA, April 10-12, 2006.

[326] D. Novikov, R. V. Yampolskiy and L. Reznik, *Artificial Intelligence Approaches for Intrusion Detection, Long Island Systems Applications and*

Technology Conference (LISAT2006). , Long Island, New York., May 5, 2006.

[327] D. Novikov., *Neural Networks to Intrusion Detection.*, MS thesis, Rochester Institute of Technology. Rochester, NY, October 2005.

[328] N. Oliver and A. P. Pentland, *Graphical models for driver behavior recognition in a SmartCar, In Proceedings of the IEEE Intelligent Vehicles Symposium* 2000.

[329] M. Orozco, Y. Asfaw, A. Adler, S. Shirmohammadi and A. E. Saddik, *Automatic Identification of Participants in Haptic Systems, 2005 IEEE Instrumentation and Measurement Technology Conference*, Ottawa, Canada 17-19 May 2005.

[330] M. Orozco, Y. Asfaw, S. Shirmohammadi, A. Adler and A. E. Saddik, *Haptic-Based Biometrics: A Feasibility Study, IEEE Virtual Reality Conference*, Alexandria, Virginia, USA, March 25-29, 2006.

[331] S. Pamudurthy, E. Guan, K. Mueller and M. Rafailovich, *Dynamic Approach for Face Recognition using Digital Image Skin Correlation, Audio- and Video-based Biometric Person Authentication (AVBPA)*, New York, July 2005.

[332] N. R. Peddisetty, *State-of-the-art Intrusion Detection: Technology, Challenges, and Evaluation, Linköping University, Department of Electrical Engineering LITH-ISY-EX-3586-2005* Available at: http://www.diva-portal.org/diva/getDocument?urn_nbn_se_liu_diva-2792-1__fulltext.pdf, 2005.

[333] A. G. Pennington, J. D. Strunk, J. L. Griffin, C. A. N. Soules, G. R. Goodson and G. R. Ganger, *Storage-based intrusion detection: Watching storage activity for suspicious behavior, Technical report CMU--CS--02--179. Carnegie Mellon University*, October 2002.

[334] T. Perrine and D. Kowarch, *Teracrack: Password cracking using TeraFLOP and PetaByte Resources*, Available at:

http://security.sdsc.edu/publications/teracrack.pdf, Retrieved December 15, 2005.

[335] J. Pierce, J. Wells, M. Warren and D. Mackay, *Conceptual Model for Graphical Authentication, 1st Australian Information Security Management Conference*, Edith Cowan University, Australia 2003.

[336] R. Plamondon and G. Lorette, *Automatic Signature Verification and Writer Identification: The State of the Art*, Pattern Recognition, 22(2) (1989), pp. 107-131.

[337] J. Planquart, *Application of Neural Networks to Intrusion Detection*, SANS Institute (2001).

[338] C. Pope and K. Kaur, *Is It Human or Computer? Defending E-Commerce with Captchas, IT Professional*, Mar/Apr, 2005, pp. 43-49.

[339] S. Porter, *Stronger Passwords through Visual Authentication: handwing, University of Glasgow.*, Available at: http://www.dcs.gla.ac.uk/~porters/thesis.pdf, Retrieved November 4, 2005.

[340] S. Pramanik, V. Sankarnarayanan and S. Upadhyaya, *Security Policies to Mitigate Insider Threat in the Document Control Domain, 20th Annual Computer Security Applications Conference*, Tucson, AZ, December, 2004.

[341] G. Prassas, K. C. Pramataris and O. Papaemmanouil, *Dynamic Recommendations in Internet Retailing, In Proceedings of the 9th European Conference on Information Systems (ECIS 2001)*, June 2001.

[342] M. Pritchard, *How to Hurt the Hackers: The Scoop on Internet Cheating and How You Can Combat It*, Information Security Bulletin (February 2001).

[343] N. Provos and D. Mazieres, *A Future-Adaptable Password Scheme, USENIX Annual Technical Conference*, Monterey, California, USA June 6-11, 1999.

[344] M. Pusara and C. E. Brodley, *User re-authentication via mouse movements*, *VizSEC/DMSEC '04: Proceedings of the 2004 ACM workshop on Visualization and data mining for computer security*, ACM Press, Washington DC, USA, 2004, pp. 1--8.

[345] F. Ramann, C. Vielhauer and R. Steinmetz, *Biometric applications based on handwriting IEEE International Conference on Multimedia and Expo (ICME '02)*, 2002, pp. 573- 576.

[346] J. Ramon, N. Jacobs and H. Blockeel, *Opponent modeling by analysing play.*, *Proceedings of Workshop on agents in computer games*, Edmonton, Alberta, Canada, 2002.

[347] N. K. Ratha, A. Senior and R. M. Bolle, *Automated Biometrics, Proceedings of International Conference on Advances in Pattern Recognition*, Rio de Janeiro, Brazil, March 2001.

[348] K. Renaud, *Quantifying the Quality of Web Authentication Mechanisms. A Usability Perspective, Journal of Web Engineering, Vol. 0, No. 0*, Rinton Press, Available at: http://www.dcs.gla.ac.uk/~karen/Papers/j.pdf, 2003.

[349] K. Renaud and E. Smith, *Jiminy: Helping Users to Remember Their Passwords, Annual Conference of the South African Institute of Computer Scientists and Information Technologists*, Pretoria, South Africa, 25-28 September 2001.

[350] B. Rhodes, J. Mahaffey and J. Cannady, *Multiple Self-Organizing Maps for Intrusion Detection*, GIT Information Technology and Telecommunications Laboratorys (1999).

[351] Z. Riha and V. Matyas, *Biometric Authentication Systems, FI MU Report Series*, 2000.

[352] S. Ross, *Is It Just My Imagination?*, Available at: http://research.microsoft.com/displayArticle.aspx?id=417, Retrieved November 4, 2005.

[353] N. Rowe, *A taxonomy of deception in cyberspace, International Conference on Information Warfare and Security*, Princess Anne, Maryland, USA, March 2006.

[354] A. D. Rubin, *Independent one-time passwords, Proceedings of the 5th Security Symposium USENIX Association*, Berkeley, CA, June 1995.

[355] T. Ruggles, *Comparison of biometric techniques*, Available at: http://www.bio-tech-inc.com/bio.htm, Retrieved: May 27, 2007.

[356] A. Y. Rui and Z. Liu, *ARTiFACIAL: automated reverse turing test using FACIAL features Proceedings of the eleventh ACM international conference on Multimedia*, 2003 pp. 295 - 298

[357] Y. Rui and Z. Liu, *Excuse me, but are you human?, Proceedings of the eleventh ACM international conference on Multimedia*, Berkeley, CA, USA 2003 pp. 462-463.

[358] Y. Rui, Z. Liu, S. Kallin, G. Janke and C. Paya, *Characters or Faces: A User Study on Ease of Use for HIPs, Proc. of 2nd Int'l Workshop on Human Interactive Proofs*, Lehigh University, Bethlehem, Pennsylvania USA, May 18-20, 2005.

[359] A. Rusu and V. Govindaraju, *A human interactive proof algorithm using handwriting recognition, Proceedings of Eighth International Conference on Document Analysis and Recognition*, 29 Aug.-1 Sept. 2005, pp. 967-971.

[360] A. Rusu and V. Govindaraju., *Handwritten CAPTCHA: using the difference in the abilities of humans and machines in reading handwritten words, Ninth International Workshop on Frontiers in Handwriting Recognition, IWFHR-9* 26-29 Oct. 2004, pp. 226- 231.

[361] M. Sabhnani and G. Serpen, *Application of Machine Learning Algorithms to KDD Intrusion Detection Dataset within Misuse Detection Context*, EECS, University of Toledo (2003).

[362] R. M. Sampson, *Reverse Turing Tests and Their Applications*, Available at: http://www-users.cs.umn.edu/~sampra/research/ReverseTuringTest.PDF, Retrieved October 8, 2006.

[363] C. Sanderson and K. K. Paliwal, *Information Fusion for Robust Speaker Verification, Proc. 7th European Conference on Speech Communication and Technology (EUROSPEECH'01)*, Aalborg, 2001.

[364] S. Schimke, C. Vielhauer, P. K. Dutta, T. K. Basu, A. D. Rosa, J. Hansen, B. Yegnanarayana and J. Dittmann, *Cross Cultural Aspects of Biometrics, Biometrics: Challenges arising from Theory to Practice*, 2004, pp. 27-30.

[365] M. Schonlau, W. DuMouchel, W.-H. Ju, A. F. Karr, M. Theus and Y. Vardi, *Computer Intrusion: Detecting Maquerades*, Statistical Science, 16 (2001), pp. 1-17.

[366] S. A. C. Schuckers, *Spoofing and Anti-Spoofing Measures, Information Security Technical Report*, 2002, pp. 56 - 62.

[367] A. Seleznyov, *An Anomaly Intrusion Detection System Based on Intelligent User Recognition. PhD dissertation*, University of Jivaskyla. Finland., 2002.

[368] A. Seleznyov and S. Puuronen, *Anomaly Intrusion Detection Systems: Handling Temporal Relations between Events, Web proceedings of the 2nd International Workshop on Recent Advances in Intrusion Detection (RAID'99)*, 1999.

[369] G. Shaffer, *Good and Bad Passwords How-To, GeodSoft*, Available at: http://geodsoft.com/howto/password/, Retrieved December 12, 2005.

[370] R. Sharman, H. R. Rao, S. J. Upadhyaya, P. Khot, S. M. and and S. Ganguly, *Functionality Defense by Heterogeneity: A new paradigm for Securing Systems, Hawaii International Conference on System Sciences (HICSS)*, Big Island, Hawaii, USA, 2004.

[371] B. A. Shawar and E. Atwell, *A chatbot system as a tool to animate a corpus*, ICAME Journal, 29 (2005), pp. 5-24.

[372] J. S. Sherif and T. G. Dearmond, *Intrusion Detection: Systems and Models Eleventh IEEE International Workshops on Enabling Technologies: Infrastructure for Collaborative Enterprises (WETICE'02)*, pp. 115.

[373] O. Shipilova, *Person Recognition Based On Lip Movements*, Available at: http://www.it.lut.fi/kurssit/03-04/010970000/seminars/Shipilova.pdf, Retrieved July 15, 2006.

[374] C. Shoemaker, *Hidden bits: A survey of techniques for digital watermarking, Independent Study EED-290*, Available at: http://www.vu.union.edu/~shoemakc/watermarking/watermarking.html, Spring 2002.

[375] M. Sicart, *On the Foundations of Evil in Computer Game Cheating, roceedings of the Digital Games Research Association's 2nd International Conference - Changing Views: Worlds in Play*, Vancouver, British Columbia, Canada, June 16-20, 2005.

[376] L. d. S. Silva, A. F. d. Santos, J. D. d. Silva and A. Montes, *A Neural Network Application for Attack Detection in Computer Networks*, Instituto Nacional de Pesquisas Espanciais (2004).

[377] P. Y. Simard, R. Szeliski, J. Benaloh, J. Couvreur and I. Calinov, *Using Character Recognition and Segmentation to Tell Computer from Humans, Seventh International Conference on Document Analysis and Recognition*, August 2003.

[378] J. H. Smith, *Playing dirty - understanding conflicts in multiplayer games, 5th annual conference of The Association of Internet Researchers*, The University of Sussex, 2004.

[379] R. E. Smith, *The Strong Password Dilemma, Authentication: From Passwords to Public Keys*, Addison-Wesley, 2002.

[380] A. Snyder, *The Poker Tournament Formula*, Cardoza, August 1, 2006.

[381] L. Sobrado and J.-C. Birget, *Graphical passwords* Available at: http://rutgersscholar.rutgers.edu/volume04/sobrbirg/sobrbirg.htm, Retrieved November 3, 2005.

[382] N. Solayappan and S. Latifi, *A Survey of Unimodal Biometric Methods, Security and Management*, Las Vegas, Nevada, USA, 2006, pp. 57-63.

[383] R. Sommer and V. Paxson, *Enhancing Byte-Level Network Intrusion Detection Signatures with Context, Proc. of 10th ACM Conference on Computer and Communications Security*, 2003.

[384] E. Spafford, *Observing Reusable Password Choices*, Available at: citeseer.ist.psu.edu/spafford92observing.html, Retrieved November 3, 2005.

[385] E. Spafford, *Opus: Preventing Weak Password Choices, Computers and Security*, Available at: citeseer.ist.psu.edu/spafford91opus.html, May 1992, pp. 273-278.

[386] E. H. Spafford and S. A. Weeber., *Software Forensics: Can We Track Code to its Authors?*, *15th National Computer Security Conference*, Oct 1992, pp. 641-650.

[387] S. M. Specht and R. B. Lee, *Distributed denial of service: taxonomies of attacks, tools and countermeasures, International Workshop on Security in Parallel and Distributed (17th ICPADS)*, September 2004, pp. 543-550.

[388] N. Stakhanova, S. Basu and J. Wong, *Taxonomy of Intrusion Response Systems, International Journal of Information and Computer Security*, 2006.

[389] E. Stamatatos, N. Fakotakis and G. Kokkinakis, *Automatic authorship attribution, in Proc. nineth Conf. European Chap. Assoc. Computational Linguistics*, Bergen, Norway, Jun. 1999, pp. 158--164.

[390] S. Standring, *Gray's Anatomy: The Anatomical Basis of Medicine and Surgery*, Churchill-Livingstone, 2004.

[391] P. T. Stanton, W. Yurcik and L. Brumbaugh, *FABS: file and block surveillance system for determining anomalous disk accesses, Proceedings from the Sixth Annual IEEE Information Assurance Workshop*, 15-17 June 2005, pp. 207 - 214

[392] T. Steffens, *Feature-based declarative opponent modelling in multi-agent systems, Master thesis, Universität Osnabrück*, 2002.

[393] S. J. Stolfo, S. Hershkop, K. Wang, O. Nimeskern and C.-W. Hu, *A Behavior-based Approach to Securing Email Systems, Mathematical Methods, Models and Architectures for Computer Networks Security*, Springer Verlag, Sept. 2003.

[394] S. J. Stolfo, C.-W. Hu, W.-J. Li, S. Hershkop, K. Wang and O. Nimeskern, *Combining Behavior Models to Secure Email Systems, CU Tech Report* Available at: www1.cs.columbia.edu/ids/publications/EMT-weijen.pdf, April 2003.

[395] P. Syverson, *A Taxonomy of Replay Attacks, Proceedings of the Computer Security Foundations Workshop VII*, Franconia NH, 1994.

[396] K. Thompson, G. Miller and R. Wilder, *Wide area Internet traffic patterns and characteristics, In IEEE Network*, November 1997, pp. 10--23.

[397] J. Thorpe, P. C. v. Oorschot and A. Somayaji, *Pass-thoughts: Authenticating with Our Minds* Available at: citeseer.ist.psu.edu/thorpe05passthoughts.html, Retrieved October 23, 2005.

[398] J. Thorpe and P. v. Oorschot, *Graphical Dictionaries and the Memorable Space of Graphical Passwords, 13th USENIX Security Symposium*, pp. 135–150.

[399] J. Thorpe and P. v. Oorschot, *Towards Secure Design Choices For Implementing Graphical Passwords, 20th Annual Computer Security Applications Conference*, Tucson, Arizona December 6-10, 2004.

[400] M. Treaster, *A Survey of Distributed Intrusion Detection Approaches*, *ArXiv Computer Science e-prints: cs/0501001*, Available at: http://arxiv.org/abs/cs/0501001, December 2005.

[401] M. O. Trujillo, I. Shakra and A. E. Saddik, *Haptic: the new biometrics-embedded media to recognizing and quantifying human patterns*, *MULTIMEDIA '05: Proceedings of the 13th annual ACM international conference on Multimedia*, ACM Press, Hilton, Singapore, 2005, pp. 387--390.

[402] W.-H. Tsai and H.-M. Wang, *Automatic singer recognition of popular music recordings via estimation and modeling of solo vocal signals IEEE Transactions on Audio, Speech and Language Processing*, Jan. 2006, pp. 330- 341.

[403] W.-H. Tsai and H.-M. Wang, *Automatic singer recognition of popular music recordings via estimation and modeling of solo vocal signals, IEEE Transactions on Audio, Speech and Language Processing*, Jan. 2006, pp. 330- 341.

[404] K. Tsipenyuk, B. Chess and G. McGraw, *Seven pernicious kingdoms: a taxonomy of software security errors*, Security & Privacy Magazine, 3(6) (Nov.-Dec. 2005), pp. 81- 84.

[405] A. Tsymbal, *The problem of concept drift: definitions and related work*, *Technical Report TCD-CS-2004-15, Computer Science Department, Trinity College* Dublin, Ireland, 2004.

[406] S. Tulyakov and V. Govindaraju, *Classifier Combination Types for Biometric Applications*, *CVPRW '06: Proceedings of the 2006 Conference on Computer Vision and Pattern Recognition Workshop*, Washington, DC, USA, 2006, pp. 58.

[407] S. Tulyakov and V. Govindaraju, *Combining Matching Scores in Identification Model*, *Proceedings of the International Conference on Document Analysis and Recognition*, Seoul, S. Korea, 2005, pp. 1151-1155.

[408] S. Tulyakov and V. Govindaraju, *Using Independence Assumption to Improve Multimodal Biometric Fusion*, in R. P. Nikunj C. Oza, Josef Kittler, Fabio Roli ed., *Multiple Classifier Systems*, Seaside, CA, USA, 2005, pp. 147-155.

[409] A. Turing, *Computing Machinery and Intelligence*, Mind, 1950, pp. 433-460.

[410] U. Uludag, S. Pankanti, S. Prabhakar and A. K. Jain, *Biometric Cryptosystems: Issues and Challenges*, *Proceedings of the IEEE*, June 2004.

[411] S. Upadhyaya, R. Chinchani and K. Kwiat, *An analytical framework for reasoning about intrusions*, *IEEE Symposium on Reliable Distributed Systems*, 2001, pp. 99-108.

[412] S. Upadhyaya and K. Kwiat, *A distributed concurrent intrusion detection scheme based on assertions*, *SCS International Symposium on Performance Evaluation of Computer and Telecommunication Systems*, July 1999, pp. 369--376.

[413] C. Vallve-Guionnet, *Finding colluders in card games*, *International Conference on Information Technology: Coding and Computing (ITCC 2005)*, 4-6 April 2005, pp. 774-775.

[414] C. Varenhorst, *Passdoodles; a Lightweight Authentication Method*, Available at: http://people.csail.mit.edu/emax/papers/varenhorst.pdf, July 27, 2004.

[415] O. D. Vel, A. Anderson, M. Corney and G. Mohay, *Mining Email Content for Author Identification Forensics*, *SIGMOD: Special Section on Data Mining for Intrusion Detection and Threat Analysis*, 2001.

[416] A. A. Velankar, *The Many Faces of Intrusion Detection System*, Available at http://www.utdallas.edu/~axv028100/courses/cs6390/paper/IDS_paper_may01.pdf, Retrieved October 7, 2006.

[417] R. N. J. Veldhuis, A. M. Bazen, J. A. Kauffman and P. H. Hartel, *Biometric verification based on grip-pattern recognition, Security, Steganography, and Watermarking of Multimedia Contents*, 2004, pp. 634-641.

[418] T. Verwoerd and R. Hunt, *Intrusion detection techniques and approaches* Computer Communications 25(15) (15 September 2002), pp. 1356-1365

[419] G. Vijayaraghavan and C. Kaner, *Bug Taxonomies: Use Them to Generate Better Tests, Software Testing Analysis & Review Conference (STAR) East*, Orlando, FL, 2003.

[420] D. Wagner and D. Dean, *Intrusion detection via static analysis, In IEEE Symposium on Security and Privacy*, 2001.

[421] S.-Y. Wang, H. S. Baird and J. L. Bentley, *CAPTCHA Challenge Tradeoffs: Familiarity of Strings versus Degradation of Images, 8th International Conference on Pattern Recognition*, 20-24 Aug. 2006, pp. 164- 167.

[422] T. Wark, D. Thambiratnam and S. Sridharan, *Person authentication using lip information, Proceedings of IEEE 10th Annual Conference. Speech and Image Technologies for Computing and Telecommunications*, 1997, pp. 153-156.

[423] C. Warrender, S. Forrest and B. Pearlmutter, *Detecting intrusions using system calls: alternative data models, Proceedings of the 1999 IEEE Symposium on Security and Privacy* Oakland, CA, USA, 05/09/1999 - 05/12/1999, pp. 133-145.

[424] N. Weaver, V. Paxson, S. Staniford and R. Cunningham, *A Taxonomy of Computer Worms, Proceedings of the 2003 ACM workshop on Rapid Malcode*, Washington, DC, October 2003, pp. 11-18.

[425] S. Webb, *A Survey of Cheating Techniques in Online Games*, Available at: http://home.cc.gatech.edu/webb/uploads/10/MiniProject3.pdf, Retrieved October 30, 2006.

[426] D. Weinshall and S. Kirkpatrick, *Passwords you'll never forget, but can't recall*, *Available at: http://www.cs.huji.ac.il/~kirk/Imprint_CHI04_final.pdf*, Retrieved October 24, 2005.

[427] D. Weirich, M. A. Sasse and *Pretty good persuasion: a first step towards effective password security in the real world, Proceedings of the 2001 workshop on New security paradigms* Cloudcroft, New Mexico 2001, pp. 137 - 143.

[428] P. Werbos, *Beyond Regression: New Tools for Prediction and Analysis in the Behavioral Sciences*, PhD thesis (1974).

[429] A. Wespi, M. Dacier and H. Debar, *Intrusion Detection Using Variable-Length Audit Trail Patterns, In Recent Advances in Intrusion Detrection (RAID)*, 2000.

[430] T. Westeyn, P. Pesti, K. Park and T. Starner, *Biometric Identification using Song-Based Eye Blink Patterns, Human Computer Interaction International (HCII)*, Las Vegas, NV, July 2005.

[431] T. Westeyn and T. Starner, *Recognizing Song-Based Blink Patterns: Applications for Restricted and Universal Access, Sixth IEEE International Conference on Automatic Face and Gesture Recognition*, 2004, pp. 717.

[432] S. Wiedenbeck, J. Waters, J.-C. Birget, A. Brodskiy and N. Memon, *Authentication Using Graphical Passwords: Basic Results*, Available at: http://clam.rutgers.edu/~birget/grPssw/susan3.pdf, Retrieved October 23, 2005.

[433] S. Wiedenbeck, J. Waters, J.-C. Birget, A. Brodskiy and N. Memon, *Authentication using graphical passwords: effects of tolerance and image choice, ACM International Conference Proceeding Series; Vol. 93, Proceedings of the 2005 symposium on Usable privacy and security* Pittsburgh, Pennsylvania, 2005.

[434] S. Wiedenbeck, J. Waters, J.-C. Birget, A. Brodskiy and N. Memon, *PassPoints: Design and Longitudinal Evaluation of a Graphical Password*

System International Journal of Human-Computer Studies, Volume 63, Issues 1-2, Elsevier Science July 2005.

[435] E. Willett, *Music Preferences, Available at: http://www.edwardwillett.com/Columns/musicpreference.htm* Retrieved October 6, 2005.

[436] S. Wilson, *ASCII Artist,* http://www.glassgiant.com/, Retrieved October 21, 2005.

[437] J. Xu, R. Lipton, I. Essa, M. Sung and Y. Zhu, *Mandatory human participation: a new authentication scheme for building secure systems, Proceedings of the 12th International Conference on Computer Communications and Networks. ICCCN 2003.* , 20-22 Oct. 2003, pp. 547-552.

[438] R. Yampolskiy, D. Novikov and L. Reznik, *Comparison of MLP and RBF in Character Recognition with Fuzzy Zoning Feature, 1st Annual Conference on Computing and Information Sciences,* Rochester, NY, January 21, 2005.

[439] R. Yampolskiy, L. Reznik and D. Novikov, *Experimental Study of the Choice Between MLP and RBF Neural Networks for Character Recognition,* IEEE – WNYIPW (2003).

[440] R. V. Yampolskiy, *Analyzing User Password Selection Behavior for Reduction of Password Space, The IEEE International Carnahan Conference on Security Technology (ICCST06),* Lexington, Kentucky, October 17-19, 2006.

[441] R. V. Yampolskiy, *Behavior Based Identification of Network Intruders, 19th Annual CSE Graduate Conference (Grad-Conf2006),* Buffalo, NY, February 24, 2006.

[442] R. V. Yampolskiy, *Behavioral Modeling: an Overview,* American Journal of Applied Sciences, Volume 5, Issue 5 (2008), pp. 496-503.

[443] R. V. Yampolskiy, *Detecting and Controlling Cheating in Online Poker*, *Fifth Annual IEEE Consumer Communications and Networking Conference (CCNC2008)*, Las Vegas, Nevada, January 10-12, 2008.

[444] R. V. Yampolskiy, *Embedded CAPTCHA for Online Poker*, *20th Annual CSE Graduate Conference (Grad-Conf2007)*, Buffalo, NY, April 13, 2007.

[445] R. V. Yampolskiy, *Enhanced Passwords for Improved Network Security*, *IEEE Upstate NY Workshop on Communications and Networks '07*, Syracuse, New York, November 9, 2007.

[446] R. V. Yampolskiy, *Feature Extraction Approaches for Optical Character Recognition*, Briviba Scientific Press, 2007.

[447] R. V. Yampolskiy, *Feature Extraction Methods for Character Recognition*, *Master's Thesis. Rochester Institute of Technology*, Rochester, NY, May 10, 2004.

[448] R. V. Yampolskiy, *Graphical CAPTCHA embedded in cards*, *Western New York Image Processing Workshop (WNYIPW)*, Rochester, New York, September 28, 2007.

[449] R. V. Yampolskiy, *Human Computer Interaction Based Intrusion Detection*, *4th International Conference on Information Technology: New Generations (ITNG 2007)*, Las Vegas, Nevada, USA, April 2-4, 2007.

[450] R. V. Yampolskiy, *Indirect Human Computer Interaction-Based Biometrics for Intrusion Detection Systems*, *The 41st Annual IEEE International Carnahan Conference on Security Technology (ICCST2007)*, Ottawa, Canada, October 9-11, 2007.

[451] R. V. Yampolskiy, *Motor-Skill Based Biometrics In Assuring Business processes, Proceedings of the 6th Annual Security Conference, Ed. G. Dhillon. Global Publishing*, Las Vegas, NV, USA. , April 11-12, 2007.

[452] R. V. Yampolskiy, *Online Poker Security: Problems and Solutions*, *North American Simulation and AI in Games Conference (GAMEON-NA2007)*, Gainesville, Florida, September 10-12, 2007.

[453] R. V. Yampolskiy, *Secure Network Authentication with PassText, 4th International Conference on Information Technology: New Generations (ITNG 2007)*, Las Vegas, Nevada, USA, April 2-4, 2007.

[454] R. V. Yampolskiy, *User Authentication via Behavior Based Passwords, The Third Annual IEEE Long Island Systems Applications and Technology Conference (LISAT2007)*, Farmingdale, New York, May 4, 2007.

[455] R. V. Yampolskiy and V. Govindaraju, *Behavioral Biometrics: a Survey and Classification*, International Journal of Biometric (IJBM). 1 (2008).

[456] R. V. Yampolskiy and V. Govindaraju, *Computer Security: a Survey of Methods and Systems*, Journal of Computer Science, Volume 3, Issue 7 (2007), pp. 478-486.

[457] R. V. Yampolskiy and V. Govindaraju, *Direct and Indirect Human Computer Interaction Based Biometrics*, Journal of Computers, Volume 2, Issue 8 (2007).

[458] R. V. Yampolskiy and V. Govindaraju, *Dissimilarity Functions for Behavior-Based Biometrics, Biometric Technology for Human Identification IV. SPIE Defense and Security Symposium*, Orlando, Florida, April 9-13, 2007.

[459] R. V. Yampolskiy and V. Govindaraju, *Embedded Non-Interactive Continuous Bot Detection*, ACM Computers in Entertainment, 5(4) (2007).

[460] R. V. Yampolskiy and V. Govindaraju, *Use of Behavioral Biometrics in Intrusion Detection and Online Gaming, Biometric Technology for Human Identification III. SPIE Defense and Security Symposium*, Orlando, Florida 17-22 April 2006.

[461] R. V. Yampolskiy, D. Novikov and L. Reznik, *Performance of MLP and RBF in Character Recognition Utilizing Fuzzy Zoning Feature, In Advancing Computing and Information Sciences in Leon Reznik (ed.)*, RIT Cary Graphic Arts Press, 2005, pp. 35-42.

[462] J. Yan, *Security design in online games, Proceedings of the 19th Annual Conference on Computer Security Applications*, Washington, DC, USA, 8-12 Dec. 2003, pp. 286- 295.

[463] J. Yan and B. Randell, *Security in Computer Games: from Pong to Online Poker, Techical Report #889, School of Computing Science, Newcastle University,* Available at: http://www.cs.ncl.ac.uk/research/pubs/trs/papers/889.pdf, Feb 2005.

[464] J. Yan and B. Randell, *A systematic classification of cheating in online games, Proceedings of 4th ACM SIGCOMM workshop on Network and system support for games (NetGames '05)*, Hawthorne, NY, 2005, pp. 1-9.

[465] J. J. Yan and H. J. Choi, *Security issues in online games The Electronic Library*, 2002, pp. 125-133.

[466] Z. Yang, X. Wei, L. Bi, D. Shi and H. Li, *An intrusion detection system based on RBF neural network, Proceedings of the Ninth International Conference on Computer Supported Cooperative Work in Design*, 24-26 May 2005, pp. 873- 875.

[467] N. Ye, *A markov chain model of temporal behavior for anomaly detection, In Proceedings of the 2000 IEEE Systems, Man, and Cybernetics Information Assurance and Security Workshop*, 2000.

[468] D. Y. Yeung and C. Chow, *Parzen-window Network Intrusion Detectors*, Sixteenth International Conference on Pattern Recognition (2002).

[469] D. Y. Yeung and Y. Ding, *Host-based intrusion detection using dynamic and static behavioral models*, Pattern Recognition, 36, pp. 229-243.

[470] A. Ypma and R. Duin, *Novelty Detection using Self-Organizing Maps*, Progress in Connectionist-Based Information Systems, vol. 2 (1998).

[471] K. Yutaka, *Behaviormetrics, Available at: http://koko15.hus.osaka-u.ac.jp/*, Retrieved October 6, 2005.

[472] Y. Zhang and D. Wang, *Research on Object-Storage-Based Intrusion Detection 12th International Conference on Parallel and Distributed Systems (ICPADS)*, 12-15 July 2006, pp. 68- 78.

[473] Z. Zhang and C. Manikopoulos, *Investigation of neural network classification of computer network attacks, Proceedings of International Conference on Information Technology: Research and Education*, 11-13 Aug. 2003, pp. 590- 594.

[474] Y. Zhu, T. Tan and Y. Wang, *Biometric Personal Identification Based on Handwriting, 15th International Conference on Pattern Recognition (ICPR'00)*, 2000, pp. 2797.

[475] U. Zurutuza and R. Uribeetxeberria, *Intrusion Detection Alarm Correlation: A Survey, In Proceedings of the IADAT International Conference on Telecommunications and Computer Networks*, 1-3 December, 2004.

INDEX